THE KIDS' SCIENCE BOOK

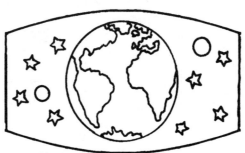

CREATIVE EXPERIENCES FOR HANDS-ON FUN

ROBERT HIRSCHFELD & NANCY WHITE

j507.8
HIR

Gareth Stevens Publishing
MILWAUKEE

A Williamson Kids Can!® Book. This library edition published by arrangement with Williamson Publishing Company.

For a free color catalog describing Gareth Stevens Publishing's list of high-quality books and multimedia programs, call 1-800-542-2595 (USA) or 1-800-461-9120 (Canada). Gareth Stevens Publishing's Fax: (414) 225-0377. See our catalog, too, on the World Wide Web: http://gsinc.com

Library of Congress Cataloging-in-Publication Data

Hirschfeld, Robert, 1942-
    The kids' science book / by Robert Hirschfeld and Nancy White.
        p. cm. — (Kids can!)
    Includes index.
    Summary: Suggests experiments involving such aspects of nature as light, trees, and water.
    ISBN 0-8368-1968-3 (lib. bdg.)
    1. Science—Experiments—Juvenile literature. [1. Science—Experiments. 2. Experiments.] I. White, Nancy, 1942-
II. Title. III. Series.
Q164.H5863   1997
507.8—dc21   97-10473

First published in this edition in North America in 1997 by
Gareth Stevens Publishing
1555 North RiverCenter Drive, Suite 201
Milwaukee, Wisconsin 53212 USA

Original © 1995 by Robert Hirschfeld and Nancy White.
This library edition published by arrangement with Williamson Publishing Company, P. O. Box 185, Charlotte, VT 05445.
Additional end matter © 1997 by Gareth Stevens, Inc.
Original paperback edition of this book is available through Williamson Publishing, 1-800-234-8791.

KIDS CAN!® is a registered trademark of Williamson Publishing Company.

Illustrations: Loretta Trezzo Braren

Printed in the United States of America

1 2 3 4 5 6 7 8 9 01 00 99 98 97

Metric Table

1 inch = 2.54 centimeters

1 foot = .3048 meter

1 pound = .4536 kilogram

1 ounce = 28.33 grams

Degrees Fahrenheit to Centigrade
    C = F-32 divided by 1.8

1 gallon = 3.784 liters

1 mile = 1.609 kilometers

1 cup = 227 grams (dry);
        240 milliliters (liquid)

In memory of my father
R.H.

For Daniel
N.W.

CONTENTS

SCIENCE ALL AROUND YOU

What picture comes to mind when you think of the word "science"? Do you think of your classroom in school? Or maybe you imagine a person in a big laboratory pouring mysterious chemicals into a test tube. Some scientists really do work in labs like that. But science doesn't happen only in laboratories or in school. Science is all around you every day in everything you do.

Want proof? Look around the kitchen. Is water steaming and bubbling as it boils on the stove? Is some fuzzy green mold growing on that forgotten piece of cheese at the back of the refrigerator? Is the heat inside the oven turning a pan of gooey batter into a delicious fluffy cake? Welcome to the world of science — right in your kitchen!

Now step outdoors. Is the wind blowing? Are there dark storm clouds overhead? Do you see a butterfly sitting on a flower, or bright autumn leaves falling from the trees? Welcome to the world of science — right outside your home!

And by the way, the most important scientific tools are with you all the time! Your abilities to see, hear, notice changes — called your powers of *observation* — and your ability to ask questions about the things that happen around you are the most important tools any scientist can have. So if you've ever wondered just what makes water boil or where those clouds came from, you've already started thinking like a scientist.

Welcome to the world of science! Have fun thinking and working like a scientist, using your powers of observation, and setting up a few scientific experiments of your own.

WHAT'S THE DIFFERENCE?

Being a scientist begins when you ask a question about what you see happening and changing around you. Why do leaves turn color in autumn? Why do things fall down instead of up? What makes day turn to night? But before you can ask questions or look for answers, you have to notice things in the first place. The more you pay attention to the things you see, hear, smell, touch, and taste in the world around you, the better scientist you will become.

Here's a science warm-up game to play with a partner. It should get your powers of observation working at top speed.

WHAT YOU NEED

Watch or kitchen timer

Blindfold (optional)

Small objects that can be moved easily

WHAT YOU DO

1 Your partner has exactly one minute to look around the room and notice as many details as possible — things like what kinds of stuffed animals are on your bed, how many sneakers are lying on the floor, or whether the lights are on or off.

2 With your partner's eyes covered, you make five changes in the room such as removing one of those sneakers, turning off the light, and so on.

3 With blindfold removed, your partner tries to pick out the five things that you changed.

4 Trade places. This time, you cover your eyes, and maybe move to a different room. After a few turns, both of you will have become better observers.

WRITE IT DOWN

Speaking of writing things down, scientists need to keep notes to help them remember their observations, findings, and thoughts. Now is a good time to start a lab book in which you can record your observations and questions, and also make notes on experiments and projects you'll be doing later on.

WHAT YOU NEED

Loose-leaf notebook and paper

Pencil

String or yarn

Crayons or markers

WHAT YOU DO

1 Set up a few pages — say four or five — that will be ready when you want to use them. You can make more later on. Here's what your lab-book pages might look like (for more on the scientific method, see pages 16 – 20):

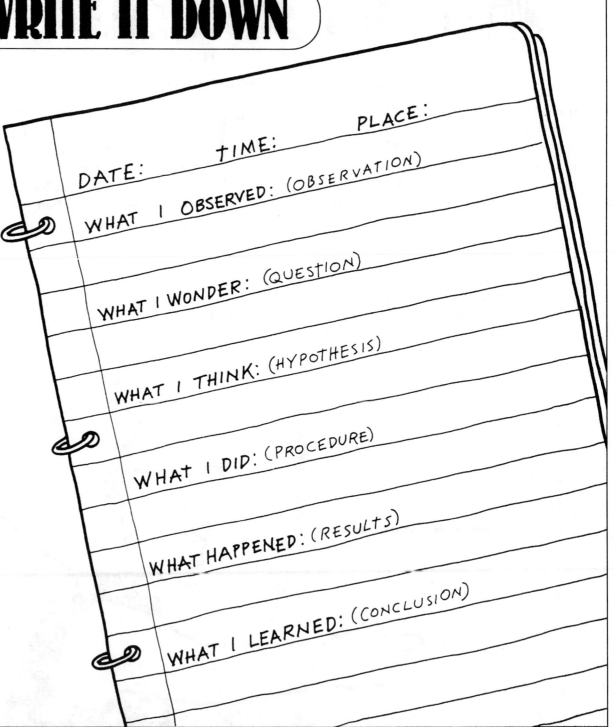

DATE: TIME: PLACE:

WHAT I OBSERVED: (OBSERVATION)

WHAT I WONDER: (QUESTION)

WHAT I THINK: (HYPOTHESIS)

WHAT I DID: (PROCEDURE)

WHAT HAPPENED: (RESULTS)

WHAT I LEARNED: (CONCLUSION)

You can use these pages for drawing pictures as well as writing things down (scientists often draw exactly what they see). Also remember that these pages are for quick notes. If you want to draw bigger pictures or write longer notes, use a blank piece of paper, and insert it into your binder.

2 To have a pencil always handy, tie one end of the string around one of the binder rings and the other end around the pencil. Keep some crayons or markers with your lab book, too, for coloring drawings.

3 If you'd like to decorate the cover of your lab book, go right ahead!

KEEP LOOKING

NATURAL WONDERS

Take your finely tuned powers of observation outdoors and use them like a scientist — to observe nature. One great way to get started is to find a quiet spot where you can sit very still and just become part of the scenery. That way, you won't frighten away any wildlife that happens to be around, and you can concentrate on keeping all your senses super-alert.

After awhile, get up and investigate what you observed. Of course, there's no telling what will happen, but here are some possibilities. It's an autumn day. You hear a rustling sound. You look in the direction of the sound and see a squirrel in a pile of dry leaves. After the squirrel scurries up a tree, you look among the leaves. There are some nuts underneath. The squirrel must have been hiding them away for winter. You notice a rock with moss growing on it. You touch the moss and feel its damp softness. When you move the rock, you see an earthworm and maybe some other creatures underneath.

Try it yourself. You're bound to find something you'll want to know more about. Write down your questions. You might just get a chance to find out some answers!

LOOK INSIDE

Lots of times, looking at things isn't enough. Scientists sometimes need to look *into* things to see what's beneath the surface. You may have dug a hole or opened a seed pod to see what was inside. Geologists break open rocks to look at their insides. And doctors use x-rays to look inside of people!

Eggs-actly!: Ask a grown-up to help you break an egg into a dish. You've seen the inside of an egg before, but this time try looking at it in a different way, examining it closely and questioning what each part is for. As you read the next paragraph, keep looking back at the egg to find the part we're talking about. Touch the parts gently to see how they feel. (Here's a good chance to use your lab book. Draw and label what you see, jot down your questions and thoughts.)

Okay, let's get started. See that yellow part in the center? That's called the *yolk*. That gooey clear part around it is called the *albumen*, sometimes called the white. Both the yolk and the albumen are food for the baby bird as it grows inside a fertilized egg. (There are, however, no baby birds growing inside the eggs in your refrigerator.) The albumen also provides a "cushion" to keep the baby from being hurt if the egg is bumped or moved. Now look for the two white, twisted "strings" at opposite sides of the yolk. These have a funny name. They're called the *chalazas* (kuh-LAY-zuhs), and they keep the yolk anchored in place so it won't be damaged.

Can you think of other things you'd like to look inside of? Here are some things that are fun to take apart to get the inside picture: an old wind-up toy, a broken watch, a broken radio, a calculator that no one uses, almost any fruit or vegetable, flower pods, broken shells on the beach. (Just remember that once you've taken something apart, you may not be able to put it together again, so be sure you ask permission first!)

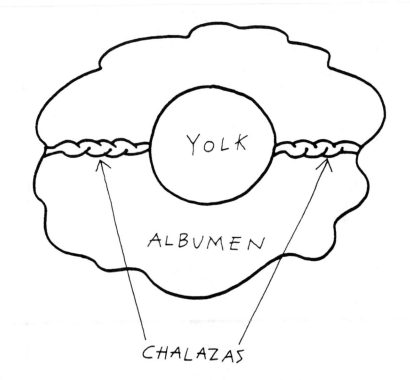

BREAK AN EGG

YOLK

ALBUMEN

CHALAZAS

MEASURING UP

In science, part of careful observation is measuring. How long is that earthworm? How heavy is this rock? How cold is the air today? How long did it take for the water in the ice tray to freeze? These are all questions about measurement.

If you don't need to be really exact, you can make pretty good guesses, or *estimates*. But to take exact measurements, scientists use special measuring tools. For example, remember the last time you went to the doctor? Did you get measured and weighed? Did the doctor take your temperature? Chances are, he or she used some measuring tools, such as a measuring stick, a scale, and a thermometer.

To see why scientists use measuring tools, get a few objects from around the house. Try guessing, or *estimating*, how long they are and how much they weigh. Then measure with a ruler and a kitchen scale. How close did you come? Even if you came close, were your guesses exact?

For a real surprise, try closing your eyes and sitting still for what you think is exactly one minute. Have someone time you with a watch that has a second hand. Did you open your eyes too soon — or not soon enough? If you guessed the right time, congratulations — you're one of the few! Now do you have a better idea about why scientists need measuring tools to get exact measurements?

TECHNIQUES & TOOLS

MEASURING THROUGH THE AGES

IN FOCUS

People who lived in ancient civilizations invented ways of measuring by using parts of the human body. Of course, their measurements weren't exact, because everybody's body is not exactly the same size! But it's interesting to know about ancient measurement because it explains a lot about how our way of measuring began. Here's how the Romans did it:

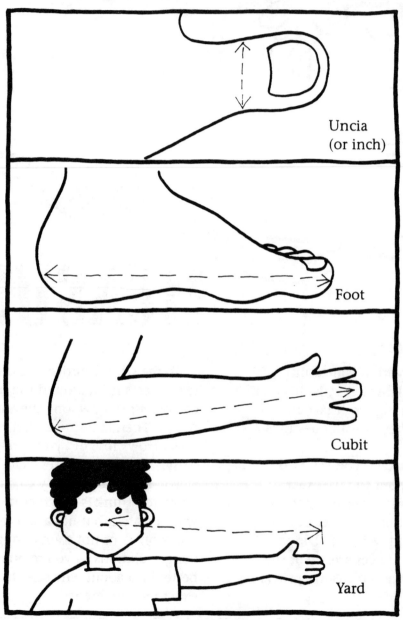

Uncia (or inch)

Foot

Cubit

Yard

Try measuring these parts of your own body. How close do your measurements come to the ones on the chart? Get a few friends to take the same measurements on themselves. Are all your thumbs and feet exactly the same size? Probably not. Now you know why people stopped using body parts and started using measuring tools.

These days, when people say an inch, they mean an inch on a ruler, not the width of someone's thumb. By a foot, they mean 12 of those ruler inches, and by a yard, they mean 3 feet or 36 inches. Whatever happened to the *cubit*? No one seems to measure things in cubits (about 18 inches) any more. (And people who use the *metric system* don't use inches, feet, and yards, either. They use centimeters and meters instead.)

MAKE A MEASURING WHEEL

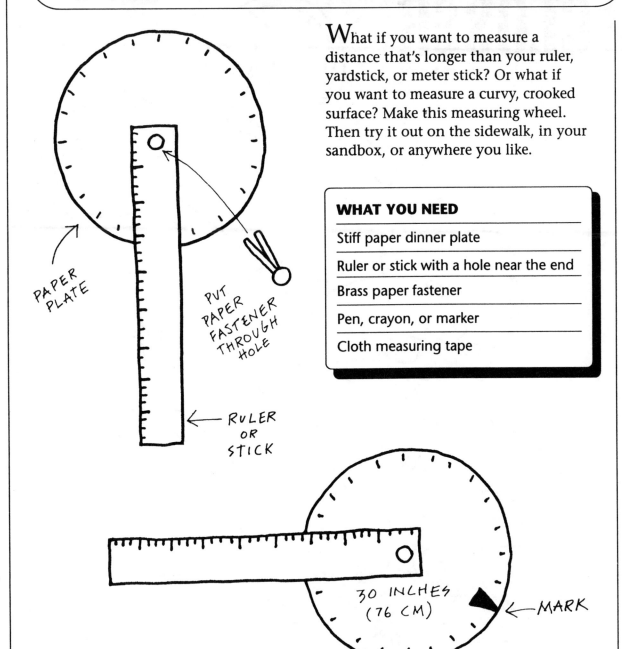

PAPER PLATE

PUT PAPER FASTENER THROUGH HOLE

← RULER OR STICK

30 INCHES (76 CM)

←—MARK

What if you want to measure a distance that's longer than your ruler, yardstick, or meter stick? Or what if you want to measure a curvy, crooked surface? Make this measuring wheel. Then try it out on the sidewalk, in your sandbox, or anywhere you like.

WHAT YOU NEED

Stiff paper dinner plate

Ruler or stick with a hole near the end

Brass paper fastener

Pen, crayon, or marker

Cloth measuring tape

WHAT YOU DO

1 Poke a hole through the center of the paper plate. Line up the hole in the plate with the hole near the end of the ruler. Insert a brass fastener through the holes and fasten the plate to the ruler.

2 Use the other end of the ruler as a handle to roll the plate across a table. If the plate wobbles, tighten the fastener or use a stiffer plate.

3 Make a bold mark near the edge of the plate. Then use the measuring tape to measure the distance all around the outside edge. Write the number of inches or centimeters on the plate, so you won't forget.

4 To use your measuring wheel, choose a surface you want to measure. Position the mark on the plate with your starting point. As you wheel the plate along, use the mark to count how many times the plate turns. At the end, multiply the number of inches or centimeters you wrote on the plate by the number of times the plate turned. (Ask a grown-up to help with the math.)

BIGGER AND CLOSER

TOOL & TECHNIQUES

What do scientists do if they want to observe very small things, like tiny insects, blood cells, or germs? They use a *magnifying glass* or a *microscope* — tools that make things look bigger.

What about things that are too far away, like a bird up high in a tree, the moon, planets, and even distant stars? They use *binoculars* or a *telescope* — tools that make things look closer.

Try it out: Try using a magnifying glass to look at the palm of your hand, a strand of yarn, or a friend's hair or tongue. In your lab book, draw a picture of exactly what you see and write down anything that surprises you.

PALM OF HAND

PIECE OF YARN

TONGUE

THE AMAZING LENS

Feel the surface of a magnifying glass. It doesn't feel flat, does it? The sides bulge outward. If you look at the glass from the side, you can see the bulges. Another word for this kind of glass is *lens*.

A *convex* lens (the kind that bulges out) makes things look bigger. A *concave* lens (one that curves inward) makes things look smaller. Lenses are used in eye glasses, in binoculars, in microscopes, and in the huge telescopes used by astronomers to look into outer space.

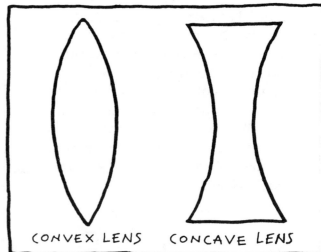

CONVEX LENS   CONCAVE LENS

ANTONIE VAN LEEUWENHOEK

◆

Besides having a name that just might be the world's most difficult to read (it's pronounced LAY-van-hook), Antonie van Leeuwenhoek is known for being the "father of the microscope." Leeuwenhoek, a Dutch amateur scientist born in 1632, didn't invent the microscope, but he was the first to make careful drawings and written descriptions of the microscopic world he saw. Through lenses he made by hand, he looked at pond water and saw tiny animals and plants. He also studied materials such as scrapings from people's teeth and blood.

◆

When you look at something under a microscope, you see amazing things. For example, what do you think grains of salt would look like? What about grains of sand? A piece of newsprint? A crayon mark? A drop of blood? If you looked at these things under the lens of a microscope, this is what you'd see:

RED AND WHITE BLOOD CELLS

CRAYON MARK

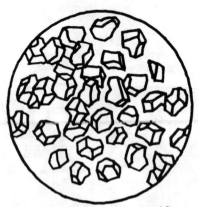

GRAINS OF SAND

IT'S A SMALL WORLD

Take a look: If there's a microscope at home or at school that you can use, here are some things you might like to look at: a drop of water from a pond, a paper-thin slice of celery, a hair, grains of sugar. First draw what you *think* you'll see. Then draw what you really see, and compare.

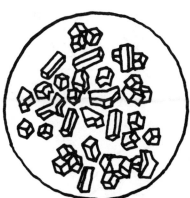

GRAINS OF SUGAR

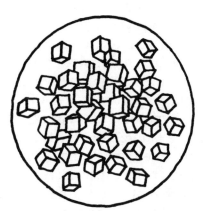

GRAINS OF SALT

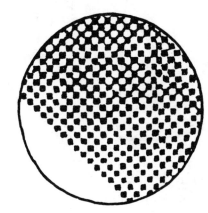

NEWSPAPER PRINT

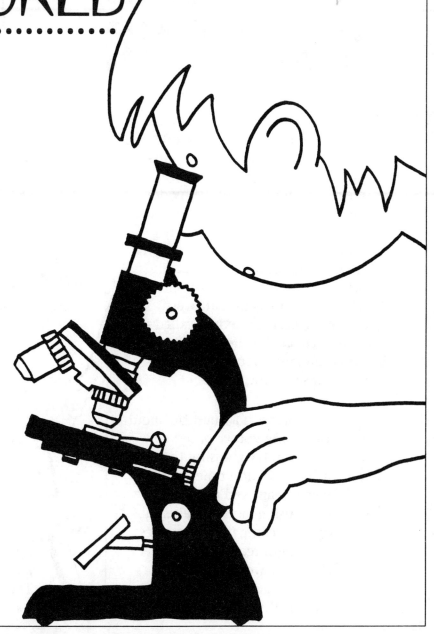

SCIENTIFIC METHOD

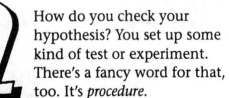

Being a good observer is the first step toward being a scientist. Start thinking and asking questions about what you observe, and you're really on your way. "Why does clothing keep us warm?" "What makes the pond freeze in winter?" "Why doesn't the ocean freeze, too?" Asking such questions and figuring out the answers is the real business of science.

How do scientists find answers? They use a special procedure called the *scientific method*, that helps them sort information and evaluate the results to come closer to the truth.

1 You start with a question about something you've observed. Then you try guessing the answer! We don't mean just guessing any old thing. We mean using facts you already know to come up with a guess that might really make sense. The fancy word for such an educated guess is *hypothesis* (hi PAH thuh sus).

2 How do you check your hypothesis? You set up some kind of test or experiment. There's a fancy word for that, too. It's *procedure*.

3 And one more thing — keep very careful notes in your lab book on everything you do and everything you find out. That's called your *data*. (Be sure you write down or draw what really happened, even if it's not what you thought would happen.) At the end, you look over all your data and think about it very hard. You think about the *results* of your procedure, or how everything turned out.

4 Finally, you draw a *conclusion*. That means you figure out whether your results agreed with your hypothesis or not. What does it all mean? What if your results *don't* agree with your hypothesis? Is your experiment a failure? Absolutely not! You learned something — just not what you expected. And in the world of science, that means success! (Your next step is a new hypothesis and another experiment to check it.)

YOU'RE GETTING WARM!

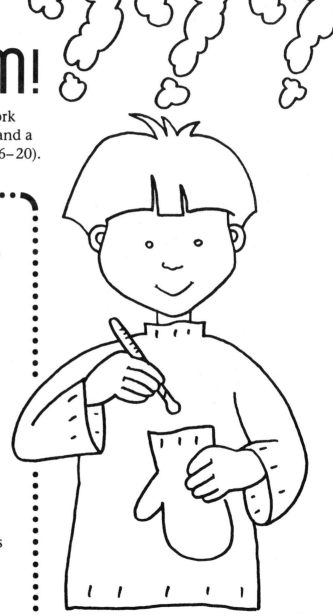

Why does clothing keep us warm, anyway? Put the scientific method to work with this fun experiment. All you need is an outdoor or room thermometer and a mitten or glove. Here's how your data will look in your lab book (see pages 16–20).

What I Observed: Mittens keep my hands warm. (This is your *observation*.)

What I Wonder: Does a mitten or glove keep me warm by raising the temperature in the mitten, which will cause a thermometer to go up? (This is your *question*.)

What I Think: I guess that there is heat in the mitten. It will make the temperature on the thermometer go up. (This is your *hypothesis*.)

What I Did: I left the thermometer on a table indoors to get the indoor air temperature. Then I put the thermometer inside the mitten to see if the temperature would go up.(This is your *procedure*.)

What Happened: The temperature didn't change at all. (These are your *results*.)

What I Learned: If there were heat in the mitten, the temperature on the thermometer would have gone up. Because the temperature didn't change, there is no heat in the mitten. There must be some other reason that mittens keep my hands warm. (This is your *conclusion*.)

IN CONTROL

Suppose that, for the mitten experiment, you just put the thermometer in the mitten right away instead of taking the air temperature first. You would have learned the temperature inside the mitten, but that wouldn't really help you answer your question. When you took the air temperature outside the mitten, and then again inside the mitten, you gave yourself *two* sets of data instead of one. And when you compared the two and found out they were the same, that's when you were able to draw your conclusion.

The part of the experiment when you took the air temperature without the mitten is called the *control*. Can you see why a control is an important part of every science experiment?

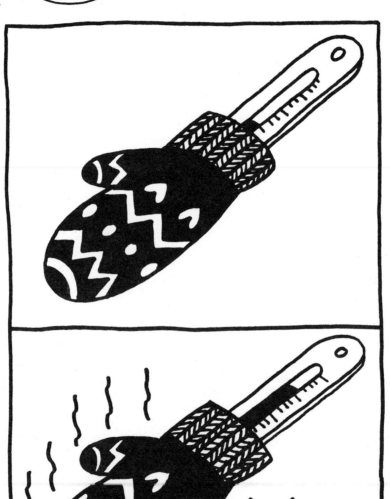

Don't change too much!:
Now, suppose that when you put the thermometer inside the mitten, you also moved the mitten to the top of a radiator. What happens to your results? Does the temperature go up? What might your conclusion be? What is wrong with this procedure?

The problem is that the thermometer went inside the mitten, PLUS it got moved to a different place. Too many things got changed. Now you don't know whether the mitten raised the temperature or the radiator raised the temperature, or both.

Things that change in an experiment are called *variables*. (Vary is another word for *change*.) A good experiment has only one variable. In the mitten experiment, the only variable should be whether the thermometer is outside or inside the mitten. Everything else has to stay the same. Can you see how putting the thermometer on the radiator throws in an extra variable? Those extra variables can really mess up your results — and lead you to the wrong conclusion.

Let's talk just a little bit more about that last part — the *conclusion*. There are no real rules for how to draw a conclusion, but the point is to put everything you observed together and try to make some sense out of it. Here's an example. Suppose you wake up one morning in December and make these three observations:

1 You're still in bed. You feel warm and cozy all over, except for your nose. That's the only part of you that's not under the covers, and it's cold.

2 You notice that the cat isn't draped over your feet, as usual. Instead, he's curled up near the radiator.

3 You come down to breakfast and there's hot, steaming oatmeal for breakfast instead of cold cereal. What's your conclusion?

If you figured out that the weather has suddenly turned colder, so you'd better wear a hat and mittens to school today, you've got the idea. (What measuring tool would you use if you wanted to check your conclusion?)

SCIENCE TALK

PUTTING IT ALL TOGETHER

BODY HEAT

If you wanted to try another procedure to find out why mittens keep your hands warm, you might try measuring the temperature in your mitten (this will be your control in this experiment) and then — for your second set of data — putting the mitten on your hand (your variable) with the thermometer still inside. Go ahead and try it. This time, your results will be different. The temperature will go up. Can you draw a conclusion from these results?

(*Conclusion: The heat is in your body — not in the mitten itself. The mitten acts as a heat trap. It keeps the heat that's already in your hand from escaping into the cold air.*)

PUT THERMOMETER INSIDE EMPTY MITTEN

(CONTROL)

THEN PUT YOUR HAND INSIDE OF MITTEN WITH THERMOMETER

(VARIABLE)

WHICH FREEZES FIRST?

MORE · SCIENCE · FUN!

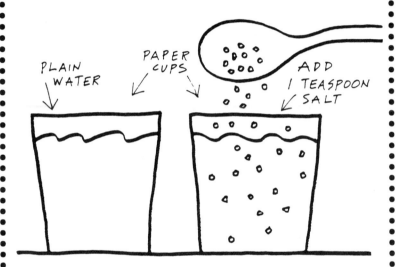

PLAIN WATER

PAPER CUPS

ADD 1 TEASPOON SALT

Now try another experiment. Use the scientific method, make sure you have a control, and then be sure there's only one variable.

Have you ever wondered why lakes and ponds freeze in winter, but not the ocean? How could you set up an experiment to find out? To help you get started, here's a hint: Place a paper cup of plain water in the freezer as your control and another paper cup of water — this one with about a teaspoon of salt mixed in — in your freezer as your variable. Keep every other detail the same. Now, you finish it up following the format on the mitten experiment.

Plain water freezes when the temperature gets down to 32° Fahrenheit (0° Celsius). When salt is mixed with water, it lowers the freezing point. That means that salty water will freeze, but it has to get colder than plain water. How much colder? That depends on how much salt is in it. The more salt in the water, the lower the freezing point, so the longer it takes to freeze.

Melt down: Here's something else you can try with salt. Get an ice cube and a salt shaker. Pour some salt on the ice cube and see what happens. Melt down! You can actually see the salt making the ice melt. Now you can see why people put salt on icy roads and sidewalks. By lowering the freezing point of the water, it makes the ice melt so cars and people won't slip and slide.

SCIENCE TALK

WHY IT WORKED

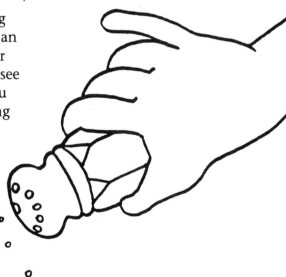

DO NOT
DISTURB—
BIRDS
NESTING

All scientists have to think about safety. Professional chemists in laboratories sometimes work with chemicals that are harmful to touch. They have to wear gloves to protect their hands and goggles to protect their eyes. Scientists your age have to think about safety, too. Here are a few simple science rules to follow:

SAFETY PATROL

TOOLS & TECHNIQUES

1 When you're observing outdoors, don't touch anything unless you know for sure what it is — or unless a grown-up tells you it's okay. That goes for plants as well as animals. (Some plants, like poison ivy, can cause skin rashes or irritations.)

When you're outdoors, let this be your motto: "Do not disturb!" Don't disturb animals or plants, and of course, never do anything to an animal that would hurt it. Observe from a distance, but don't move or touch it.

2 Never taste anything or put anything into your mouth from a science experiment or that you find when observing outdoors.

3 Fire, sharp cutting tools, using the stove or any electrical appliances are absolutely not allowed unless a grown-up is helping you.

4 Remember to protect your eyes. Good scientists wear protective goggles so things won't splatter into their eyes. Never look directly into the sun or into a very bright light. And don't touch or rub your eyes with your hands unless they're clean.

5 Protect your clothes. When you're doing crafts or science activities, wear a lab coat over your clothing. (A smock or a big old shirt with sleeves rolled up will do just fine.)

6 Don't forget the safety of the environment. Don't waste. Use recycled materials whenever possible, and re-use your supplies as much as you can.

PLANT POWER

Did you know that without plants there would be no life on earth? Just think about what we need in order to live. One thing we need is *food*. All our food comes from plants or from animals that eat plants.

Another thing we couldn't live without is air — especially *oxygen*, the part of the air our bodies need most. Did you ever wonder why the oxygen in the air doesn't get used up? The answer is that plants breathe, too, but they use carbon dioxide, the part of the air we don't need, and they give off the oxygen that we do need! So we get our oxygen from plants, too.

In addition, we depend on plants for a lot of the materials we use for building houses (wood) and for much of our clothing (cotton) — even for the paper (wood fiber) this book is printed on. Does the wool for your sweater come from plants? In a way it does, because wool comes from sheep, and sheep depend on plants for their food.

Now that you know that we get food, air, shelter, and clothing from plants, you have a good idea of just how important plants are. So, let's have some fun with plant power.

AMAZING LITTLE PACKAGES

NATURAL WONDERS

Seeds are like amazing little packages; they come complete with a tiny plant called an *embryo*, its food supply, and a protective carrying case called a *seed coat*. To get a good look at the inside of a seed, soak some dry lima beans in water and carefully split them lengthwise. You can see the little tiny plant curled up on one side of the bean. The rest of the bean is filled with food for the tiny plant — or for whatever person or animal eats the bean!

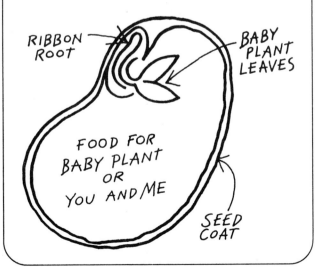

RIBBON ROOT

BABY PLANT LEAVES

FOOD FOR BABY PLANT OR YOU AND ME

SEED COAT

SPROUT ART

You don't need soil to make seeds sprout; use a wet sponge, and watch them pop out!

WHAT YOU NEED

New sponge

Scissors

Mustard seeds (from the supermarket spice section)

Plastic wrap (recycled)

Spray bottle (rinse and clean thoroughly)

WHAT YOU DO

1 Cut the new sponge into any shape you like — a circle, a heart, a star — it's up to you! Soak it in water and then squeeze it. You want the sponge to be wet, but not dripping.

2 Place the sponge on a plate or dish; sprinkle with the seeds, covering the top of the sponge evenly.

3 Cover the dish with plastic wrap every night to keep the sponge moist, and unwrap it during the day, placing in plenty of sunlight. Keep the sponge damp by spraying a water mist over it daily.

4 The seeds will soon sprout and grow. Within 12 days, your sponge will be a tiny garden of mini-mustard plants. Taste a few of the small plants; they're perfectly safe. Do you notice a mustardlike flavor? They add a nice bit of crunch and spice to a sandwich.

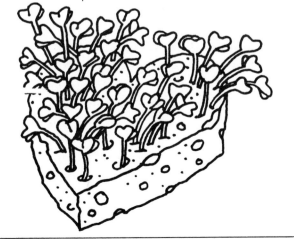

HOW'D THEY DO THAT?

How do seeds sprout on a sponge — without soil to grow in? Since seeds carry their own food supply, they don't need nourishment from soil to get started. All they need to sprout, or *germinate*, are water, sunlight, and the right temperature.

When water reaches a seed, the tiny plant inside splits the protective seed coat and starts to grow. It develops roots to take in water and sends out tiny branches and leaves that absorb sunlight. Once it uses up its original food supply the plant needs roots and leaves to help make its own food so it can keep growing.

FANCY FLOWERS

Want to make a bouquet of many colors? Here's how to make amazingly colorful carnations without any paint or markers! For a faster color change, leave the carnations tightly wrapped in the refrigerator overnight. Then the thirsty flowers will take in the colored liquid more quickly.

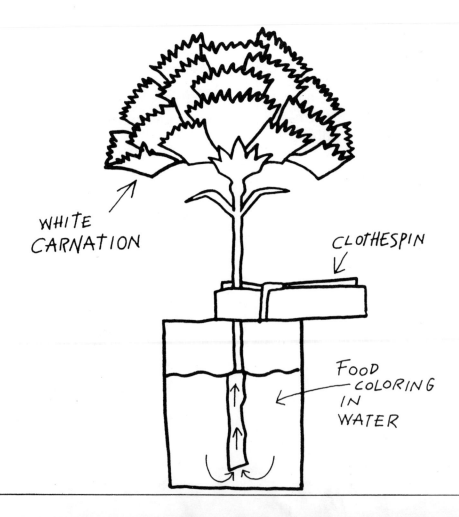

WHITE CARNATION

CLOTHESPIN

FOOD COLORING IN WATER

WHAT YOU NEED

White carnations, 1 or 2

Small, clear glass

Water

Vegetable food coloring

Sharp knife (to be used by a grown-up)

Spring-type clothespin or large paper clip

WHAT YOU DO

1 Pour some food coloring into a small glass. Mix in a very small amount of water (use more food coloring than water).

2 Cut a carnation stem so it reaches to the bottom of a glass and just rises above the rim a few inches. Prop the flower up in the glass with a\clothespin placed across the glass rim. Within hours, the flower will turn the same color as the food coloring. (This also works well with Queen Anne's Lace and other white flowers.)

3 Want to make a two-color carnation? Put different colors of food coloring in two separate glasses. Ask a grown-up to carefully slit a carnation stem lengthwise, leaving both halves attached to the base of the flower. Put the glasses side-by-side and set the flower with one-half stem in each glass. Support with a clothespin. After several hours, you'll have a two-color carnation.

PLANT A TREE AND BREATHE EASIER!

IN FOCUS

Did you know that people everywhere need trees in order to live? That's because these natural beauties give off the life-sustaining oxygen we need to breathe. But that's not all. Trees also shade and shelter people and animals from the sun and the harsh weather. During the winter months, deer rely on trees to protect them from heavy snow and cold winds.

It's for these reasons and more that we need to protect the trees we already have and encourage them to keep on growing. So what can you do to help? Start by planting a tree from a local nursery each year on Arbor Day, which is celebrated each spring. In 1872, J. Sterling Morton persuaded the Nebraskan government to start a tree-planting program, and one million trees were planted on that first Arbor Day!

SUNSHINE

WATER AND MINERALS GO UP THE TRUNK

WATER AND MINERALS GO UP THE ROOTS

WATER + MINERALS + SUNLIGHT + CHLOROPHYLL = FOOD

WHERE'S THE ACTION?

Even though we usually think of water traveling downward, your carnation changed color because its stem carried liquid upward. This process is called *capillary action*, and it happens when a liquid naturally moves up a very narrow tube. Thanks to capillary action, any plant stem can carry water up from the roots to the highest leaves and branches. The stem of your carnation contains many narrow, tubelike veins that work like this. And, the trunk of a giant redwood tree, hundreds of feet tall, works the same way!

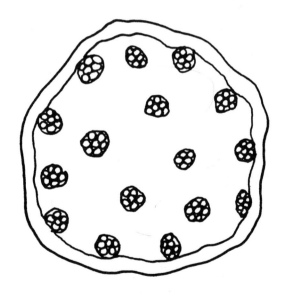

PLANTS WITH SLENDER STEMS HAVE SMALLER, SCATTERED BUNDLES OF TUBES OR CAPILLARIES.

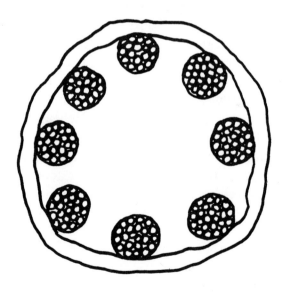

TREES AND WOODY PLANTS HAVE LARGE BUNDLES OF TUBES OR CAPILLARIES IN A CIRCLE.

SUPER SCIENTIST

WORKING FOR PEANUTS

•

One of the great things about science is that one person's research can sometimes help a nation of people. And in the case of African-American, George Washington Carver, the son of Southern slaves who grew up during the late 1800s, that's just what happened! As a boy, he was fascinated by plants and spent much of his time studying and observing how they could be used to help people. He learned a lot by walking in the wild and by asking himself questions about the things he found in nature.

Carver helped Southern farmers — both black and white — to prosperity by persuading them to grow plants, such as peanuts, that enriched the soil instead of draining it of its nutrients, as cotton did. He, then, developed over 300 products that could be made from peanuts — including everything from peanut oil soap to peanut brittle!

•

MAKING WATER CLIMB UPWARDS

Try this experiment to see capillary action at work. (Please wear a smock to protect your clothes.) The narrower a tube is, the better capillary action works. The water-carrying tubes in plant stems are much narrower than the tube you will make, so even the tallest trees can send water from their roots to their top branches and leaves.

WHAT YOU NEED

Plastic wrap, 2"-wide (5 cm) strip

Thin knitting needle

Tape

Food coloring, water

Glass

KNITTING NEEDLE

WRAP PLASTIC STRIP AROUND KNITTING NEEDLE

2" WIDE STRIP OF PLASTIC WRAP

WHAT YOU DO

1 To make a narrow tube, wind the plastic-wrap strip around the knitting needle several times, fasten with tape, and pull out the needle. Make sure it's open at both ends by blowing through it.

2 Working over newspaper, pour some food coloring and a little water into a clear glass and dip the end of the tube into the dye. The dye should climb up the tube *above* the level of the liquid in the glass.

3 For fun, try several tubes in different glasses filled to different levels with food coloring.

PUT PLASTIC-WRAP TUBE IN THE GLASS OF DYE SOLUTION. THE LEVEL OF LIQUID IN THE TUBE WILL BE <u>HIGHER</u> THAN THE LEVEL OF LIQUID IN THE GLASS.

LIQUID IN TUBE →

LIQUID LEVEL IN GLASS

SEEDS ARE SURVIVORS!

Some seeds, especially from desert plants, can survive an amazingly long time without water. Desert wild flower seeds, such as cream cups of the Sonoran Desert in southern Arizona and Mexico, can last for 5 or 6 months without the water needed to germinate. When water from a rainstorm or flash flood finally reaches them, they sprout. Then, they grow incredibly fast, so they can make new seeds before the desert dries out once again. Pretty amazing little seeds, aren't they?

SUNLIGHT

OXYGEN

CARBON DIOXIDE

SCIENCE TALK

GREEN IS FOR GROWING

Most plants make their own food. To do this, they must have sunlight, plus water and minerals that are taken in from the soil through the roots. The sunlight enables the plants to make a green chemical called *chlorophyll* (KLOR-o-fil). The chlorophyll, through a process called *photosynthesis*, then enables the plants to give off oxygen, produce their food, — and you guessed it — keep themselves green!

So, plants need sunlight to perform photosynthesis, thereby making their food and staying green. Well, don't take our word for it! As a curious scientist, you might want to prove this yourself.

Create your own experiment following the scientific method (see pages 16 – 20). To help you get started, we suggest that you take two seedlings of bean plants (or whatever you have handy). Now, remember that you want one control (one plant in sunlight) and only one variable (one plant in the dark). Everything else (kind of soil, amount of water, room temperature) must be exactly the same for both plants. Check on your plants frequently, water them equally and regularly, and write down or draw your procedure and results. What conclusion can you draw from your experiment? What did you learn about photosynthesis?

CREATE YOUR OWN EXPERIMENT

EGGHEADS

Show off your green thumb with these cute little planters.

WHAT YOU NEED

Eggs

Markers

Potting soil

Grass seed

Construction paper

Tape

WHAT YOU DO

1 Draw a funny face on an egg-shell. Gently tap off the end of the shell that is the top of the head. Shake out contents into a bowl and set aside for cooking scrambled eggs or a batch of cookies.

2 Fill the shell gently with soil. Make a base for the egghead by cutting a 1" (2.5 cm) strip of construction paper and taping it into a circle 1½" (4 cm) in diameter. The shell will stand upright in the ring.

3 Plant some grass seed in the soil and mist with water every other day, keeping the soil damp, but not soaking. Place the egghead in sunlight. In about a week, you can give your egghead a high-fashion haircut or let it grow wild.

FORMING
TUBER

TUBER

LATERAL BUD
OR EYE

NATURAL
WONDERS

A POTATO SURPRISE

A potato is actually an underground part of a potato plant's stem, called a *tuber*. Potatoes carry their seeds right on them; we call the potato's seeds, *eyes*. The inside of the potato — the part we eat — is actually food stored by the plant to feed its seeds when they begin to grow. That's why potatoes are so nourishing to us when we eat them.

THEY GROW BELOW

Every plant needs water to germinate its seed as you've seen, but some plants, such as the water lily, actually grow in very deep water. A water lily's roots grow in the muddy bottom of a shallow pond or swamp, and its long, narrow stem reaches all the way up to the surface of the water. A "field" of pink and white water lilies floating on the surface of a clear pond is one of nature's most beautiful sights.

In swamps, or *wetlands*, you can see water lilies and other amazing plants, too. Wetlands may look lush, but for plants, they're not a great place to grow up! The water has too much acid and the soil is low in the minerals the plants need.

Over a very long time, wetland plants such as water lilies have made special changes (*adaptations*) to survive in their difficult environment. The leaves and flowers of water lilies float on the water, so their tiny pores, which are on the underside of most leaves, are on the *tops* of water lily leaves. Some wetland plants even get minerals by eating insects (see pages 40 – 41).

LOVELY LILIES

When you help set the table, do it in a special way.

WHAT YOU NEED

One square paper or cloth napkin per lily

Optional: green construction paper, scissors, and paper fasteners

WHAT YOU DO

1 It is important that the napkin be square — the same length on each side — when unfolded. Small paper napkins are the easiest to use.

2 You will be making three sets of folds. For the first set, fold each of the four corners of the opened napkin into the center. Now, you have a small square.

3 Next, fold in the corners again, making a smaller square.

4 Then, turn the napkin over. Fold the corners into the center one more time. You have an even smaller square.

START WITH A SQUARE NAPKIN

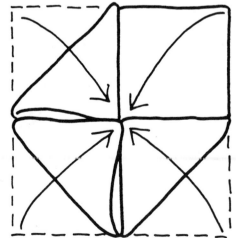

FOLD 4 CORNERS INTO THE CENTER

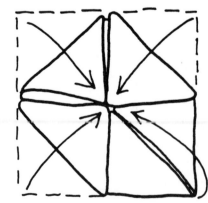

REPEAT WITH SMALLER SQUARE

TURN OVER— FOLD CORNERS TO THE CENTER

To make the petals, hold your folded napkin in place with one hand in the center. With your other hand, bend one of the corners toward the center. You will see a pointed flap underneath. Lift the flap with your fingers, while you push your thumb on the bent-up corner. When you've done all four corners, your lily will have four petals.

Turn over your almost-finished lily. Pull out the four pointed corners in the center, making four more petals.

To add green lily pads, cut out a scalloped circle a little bigger than the lily from green construction paper. Place the lily on the lily pad, and stick a paper fastener through the middle of both, or glue in place.

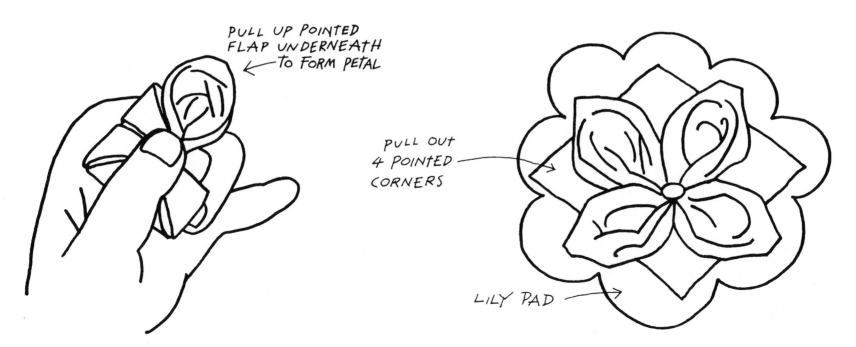

PULL UP POINTED FLAP UNDERNEATH
←— TO FORM PETAL

PULL OUT 4 POINTED CORNERS

LILY PAD →

GULP!

....

No, it isn't science fiction. Some plants actually — gulp! — eat bugs, not instead of performing photosynthesis for food, but for the nitrogen that plants need. And, since they can't chase the creatures, they make the creatures come to them!

The Venus's-flytrap, as you might guess from its name, is an insect-eating plant that grows in the wet-lands of North and South Carolina. Its leaves form little hinged traps. When an insect lands on a leaf, it brushes against leaf "trigger hairs," causing a reaction in the plant similar to nerve impulses in animals, and the trap closes. Struggles by the insect cause the plant to secrete fluids that break down the insect for digestion.

Some *carnivorous* (the word means "meat-eating") plants drown their prey in pitcher-shaped leaves full of water mixed with digestive juices; others have sticky tentacles to entangle victims. Some of these plants actually snare tiny reptiles, amphibians, and rodents, as well as insects. The horned bladderwort lures insects with tendrils that look like

the insects' favorite food. An insect will spot what looks like a meal...and become a meal for the plant!

Meet my carnivore: You don't have to live in North or South Carolina to see a Venus's-flytrap. Many greenhouses and plant stores have them for you to purchase and nurture at home. (Don't try to transplant them from the wild as they rarely survive.) Just place your plant in a bright sunny place and keep it healthy by watering it well and feeding it a few insects each day. Never overfeed your plant or give it meat, because the salt the meat contains can hurt the plant.

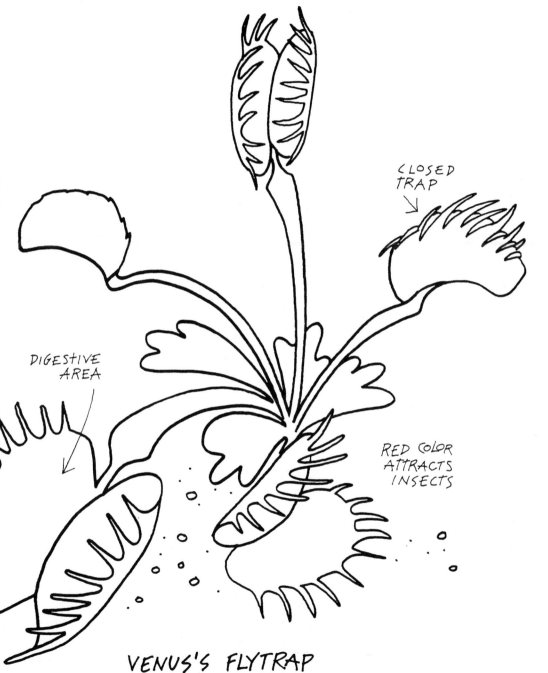

CLOSED TRAP

DIGESTIVE AREA

RED COLOR ATTRACTS INSECTS

TOOTH

VENUS'S FLYTRAP

MORE · SCIENCE · FUN!

A GARDEN WITHOUT SOIL

While water lilies may thrive in "water up to their necks," would you believe that some soil-loving plants are grown in huge greenhouses in water only — without any soil? *Hydroponics* is the science of growing plants without soil, mostly in water. *Hydro* in Greek means "water," and *ponics* means "work." A variety of plants, including wheat, potatoes, tomatoes, and beans, have been grown using hydroponic gardening. Small stones keep the plants upright in the water. Most hydroponic gardens are found indoors, so plants receive artificial light. Nutrients are pumped through the water to feed the plants.

Grow your own: You can grow some spring bulbs with water, pebbles or marbles, and sunlight. Fill a shallow bowl with pebbles. Set a few bulbs such as narcissus or paperwhites into the pebbles, root-end down, and add water. Place near a sunny window. Keep the pebbles moist, but not soaking (you don't want the bulbs to rot), and in about two to three weeks your hydroponically grown bulbs will have sprouted, soon to bloom!

CRAFTY CREATURES

Would you believe there's a kingdom on Earth you can visit no matter where you live — in the country or the city? This kingdom is filled with wonderful creatures ranging from a furry giant panda to a graceful, crawling spider to a whale as long as three school buses lined up end-to-end — to you! Our world just wouldn't be the same without this kingdom.

By now you've probably guessed this wonderful place is none other than the *animal kingdom*. (Plants have their own kingdom, called — you're right! — the *plant kingdom*. And, there are three other kingdoms for things like bacteria, small one-celled creatures, and molds.)

You may wonder, though, if animals can be so different from one another, why do they all belong to the same kingdom? All animals have three things in common.

1 All animals move around. (Plants stay in one spot once their seed germinates.)

2 Animals find their food — rather than make their own food as plants must do in photosynthesis. (Remember that even carnivorous plants still perform photosynthesis. See pages 40 – 41.) In fact, having to find food is the reason animals need to move.

3 Animals, unlike bacteria and one-celled creatures that are so small you can't even see them without a microscope, are made up of many tiny cells that all work together to keep the animal alive.

No matter how different animals seem — even a cuddly kitten and a jellyfish — they all have these three characteristics in common.

As you're having fun learning more about these crafty creatures, think about the many different kinds of animals there are in the world. How does each one help make our world a wild and wonderful place?

A KINGDOM OF THEIR OWN

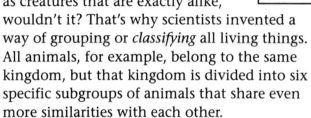

All animals aren't exactly the same, of course. Some animals have a backbone, while others don't; some, like dogs, have hair; others, like snakes, have scales. It would be silly to group snakes and dogs together as creatures that are exactly alike, wouldn't it? That's why scientists invented a way of grouping or *classifying* all living things. All animals, for example, belong to the same kingdom, but that kingdom is divided into six specific subgroups of animals that share even more similarities with each other.

Each of these six groups divides the previous group into smaller, more specific groups with shared characteristics.

Kingdom

Phylum

Class

Order

Family

Genus

Species

You belong to the genus *Homo* and the species *sapiens*, so all humans are known as *Homo sapiens*. How many species of animals do you think there are? Would you believe there are more than one million different species!

GROUPING IT ALL TOGETHER

You can come up with your own system of classifying, or grouping, things, just like a scientist. Find about 10 different items around the house or school. You can use buttons, paper clips, crayons, macaroni — anything really.

How are the items *alike* and *different* from each other? Try grouping together items that are similar in some way — such as by color, size, material, or scent.

Now, get 6 to 10 new items that you can eat. How might you further break down that group? Are some foods sweet and others salty or sour? Are some eaten at breakfast, others for snacks, and still others best for dinner? Maybe your classifying system would go like this: Food, Desserts, Sweet, Fruit, Red. Thus everything that is Sweet is also a Dessert, but not all sweets are Fruit, and not all fruits are Red. That's how the scientific classification system works: everything in a subgroup shares characteristics with the group above it, but not necessarily with all the groups below it.

A classifying hunt: Want to have some fun with a few friends? Go on a classifying scavenger hunt. The only rule is to bring back 15 very different items. One item must come from each of the following 10 places: a desk, under a tree, the refrigerator, under your bed (or in your cubby at school), a puddle or ditch, a garden or flowerpot, on a person's head, a broom closet, under a cushion, in a coat pocket. You choose the other five places. Now, sort the items into two or more kingdoms, and then begin classifying them even further. Can you and your friends agree on how to classify things?

SCIENCE TALK

INSIDE OR OUT

Animals are divided into two large groups. One is the phylum *Chordata* that contains all animals with backbones, called *vertebrates* (VURT-uh-brayts). The animals without backbones, called *invertebrates*, make up several different *phyla* (plural of phylum), including *Arthropoda, Mollusca,* and others containing worms and sponges. Play a game with yourself, a friend, or at the dinner table. Take turns naming an animal and deciding whether it is a vertebrate or an invertebrate? How would you classify an earthworm, a lobster, a crocodile? What about insects, or a turtle?

WILD AT HEART

♥

Lots of times, scientists must do incredible things to answer life's difficult questions — and sometimes the answers take years to find! Just think of English zoologist Jane Goodall who spent 30 years living in Tanzania, Africa with a community of chimps! Goodall slept, ate, and played with the apes — she even learned their language.

"Working in the field," as it's often called, helped Goodall figure out how chimps behave. And thanks to her amazing research, we know chimps and humans have lots in common, including the ability to make and use tools. Living in the wild wasn't always easy for Goodall, but she couldn't have done her important research any other way. Now that's dedication!

♥

WHOOOOO'S AWAKE?

Scientist Jane Goodall used the basic tools of science in her research — observation and recording accurate data. There is really no better way to learn about the world around you.
A night to listen and look: Ask a grown-up to join you in a night of listening and looking on a clear night. Bundle up, if it is cold outside, and bring a blanket to sit on. The materials you will need are a flashlight covered with red plastic wrap (so your night vision won't be spoiled by the bright light), a notepad, and a pencil. A stopwatch is nice if you have one.

Now, set yourself up to make some serious nighttime observations. First, get used to your surroundings. Sit quietly. What do you hear? What do you see? Write down or draw a picture of everything you hear in five minutes. Put a check mark next to it each time you hear or see the same thing. Is there a lot happening? Are you looking carefully — at the ground and the sky? The more closely you look and listen, the more you will see and hear. Remember that observation involves thinking about what you notice. Compare notes with a friend. *Describe* what you observed. Did you observe the same things?

SCIENCE TALK

A WHALE OF A MAMMAL

It is tempting to think of whales as fish because they both live in the water and they both are vertebrates. These enormous creatures of the sea may look like fish, but whales are actually *mammals* — just like dogs, horses, bats, and you! Mammals are a class in the *animal kingdom* in the *phylum* with vertebrates to which humans also belong. They give birth to live babies and nurse them with milk, and all mammals have some hair.

NATURAL WONDERS

A HEAVY COAT

Many whales live in polar waters with very cold temperatures. Since whales are mammals and are warm-blooded, you may wonder how they keep warm in the icy water. In fact, whales have a coat of fat under their skin, called *blubber*, that's over a foot thick!

Imagine what it would be like if you could hold your breath for over an hour! It sounds almost impossible, but that's exactly what many kinds of whales can do. Although whales live their whole lives in water, they must come to the surface to breathe. Whales breathe out or "spout" air and water from a *blowhole*, an opening on top of their heads.

What's another mammal that can stay underwater a long time? A beaver can stay underwater for as long as 15 minutes. What about humans? Well, most humans can only hold their breath comfortably for 15 – 20 seconds! How long can you hold your breath?

TAKE A DEEP BREATH
....

HUMPBACK WHALE

ORIGAMI WHALE

Despite the enormous size of most whales, they are very beautiful and graceful, as they glide and dive in the water. Origami, the Japanese art of paper-folding, is also very beautiful and graceful. Make an origami whale to appreciate the beauty of the whale and of this art.

WHAT YOU NEED

Black construction paper, 8" (20 cm) square

Scissors

Tape or glue

WHAT YOU DO

1 Lay the paper down in a diamond shape. Fold the two opposite sides so the edges meet in the center.

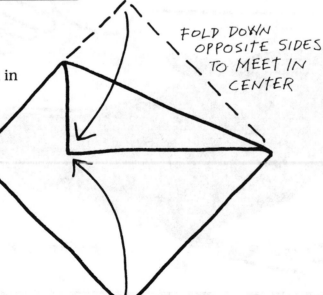

FOLD DOWN OPPOSITE SIDES TO MEET IN CENTER

2 Fold the top point down to meet the folded edges.

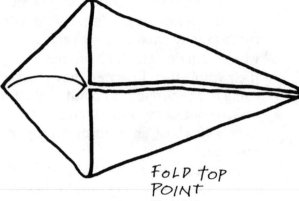

FOLD TOP POINT DOWN

3 Fold in half horizontally.

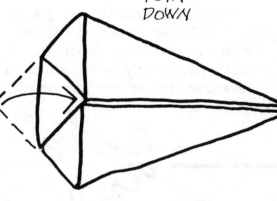

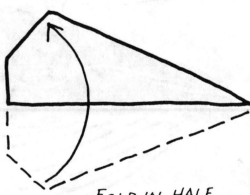

FOLD IN HALF HORIZONTALLY

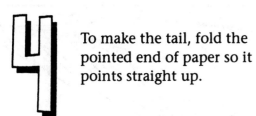

To make the tail, fold the pointed end of paper so it points straight up.

Make a 1" (2.5 cm) cut in the fold of the tail. Fold down the two parts so they spread out flat.

LIFE IN THE BALANCE

IN FOCUS

For the most part, nature's creatures are able to live and hunt in balance with one another. Often the number of babies born each year nearly balances the number of adults that die. But what happens if more animals die each year than are born? And what if the places where they live become polluted?

Sadly, these are just the sort of things that have happened to blue whales — the largest animal ever to live on Earth (much bigger than the biggest dinosaurs). These enormous sea beauties have become an *endangered species*, which means there are so few of them living in the sea that we are in danger of losing them forever! How could this have happened? Well, for years and years, whales were hunted (and still are in some places) for their blubber, to make oil perfect for lamp fuel. The whales' bones were used for art carvings.

Luckily, environmental groups are working to save thousands of miles of ocean so that whales have a safe place to eat, breed, and live in balance again. In these parts of the ocean, it is illegal to hunt whales.

AMAZING BUT TRUE

COLD AS A FISH

How are fish able to live in cold water and not freeze to death? Fish are *cold-blooded* animals, which means they have a built-in system that allows their body temperature to change, or *adapt*, to the temperature of the water they live in. So as a pond's warm summer water begins to turn colder with autumn and winter, a fish's body temperature changes right along with the water in the pond. If you could measure a fish's body temperature, it might change from 70° F (21.2° C) to 50° F (10° C). A fish swimming in the frigid Arctic might have a very low temperature while another swimming around the equator would have a very high temperature.

If you take your own temperature on a sweltering hot day in summer and then on a freezing cold day in winter, it always stays about the same, 98.6° F (37° C) (unless you're sick with a fever). That's because humans and many other animals including all *mammals* are *warm-blooded*; their bodies — wherever they live — always stay about the same temperature. That's why humans wear coats, hats, and mittens on cold days, and t-shirts and shorts on hot days. They have to find ways to keep cool or to warm up, because their body temperature — unlike a fish's — doesn't change much at all.

SOMETHING FISHY

DORSAL FIN

TAIL

GILL COVER

VENTRAL FIN →

← ANAL FIN

OVERLAPPING SCALES →

Fish are vertebrates that spend their whole lives in water, where they swim, breathe, eat, and even sleep beneath its surface. If you've ever waded in shallow water where fish hang around, you already know how quick these little swimmers are. So how do they move so fast? Well, most fish have bodies with a *streamlined* shape — sort of like a long, narrow torpedo — that lets them move easily through the water. A fish swims with its tail, which moves or propels it forward. The fins on its sides, back, and belly, help it to steer like the rudder of a boat.

Fish usually have one eye on either side of their heads and can see left and right at the same time. But unlike many living things, fish don't have any eyelids so they sleep with their eyes open!

Besides being quick swimmers, fish have an ingenious way of avoiding enemies. Their skin is covered with a slippery slime that makes them hard to catch. And over their skin, they have tough overlapping scales, much like armor. Sometimes a fish's body is camouflaged to blend right into its surroundings, so enemies don't even notice it as it swims by.

A CURIOUS BUNCH

NATURAL WONDERS

You can find fish wherever there's fresh or salt water — in oceans, rivers, lakes, and ponds. They come in all kinds of sizes, shapes, and fabulous colors.

The Deep-Sea Angler has a long growth on its head. The end of it glows in the dark, deep water where it lives. When smaller fish swim up close to look at the light, the angler fish gobbles them up!

The Black Swallower can swallow fish twice its size. How's that for gulping down your food!

The Anableps has eyes that are divided in half. The top half sees things above the surface of the water and the bottom half sees what's going on below. Sounds like a built-in periscope!

The Porcupine Fish gets its name from the sharp spines that cover it. It frightens its enemies by filling up with water until it looks like a spine-covered balloon.

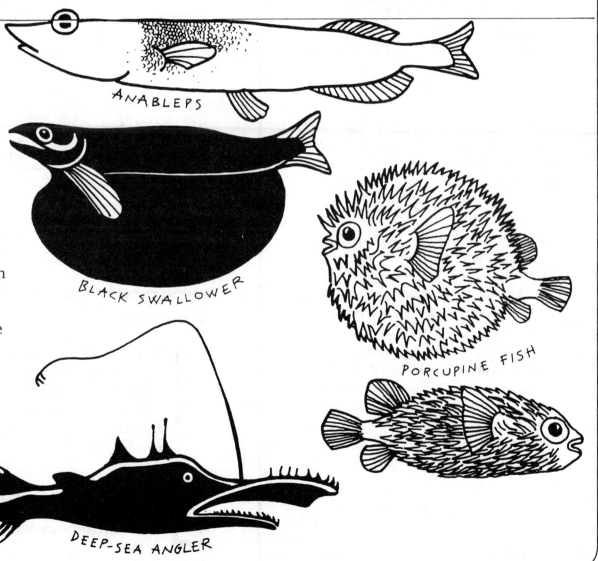

ANABLEPS

BLACK SWALLOWER

PORCUPINE FISH

DEEP-SEA ANGLER

EXPLORER OF THE SEAS

★

If you've ever opened your eyes underwater, you've seen for yourself just how different the world looks beneath the water's surface. Well, French oceanographer Jacques Cousteau felt so strongly about the beauty of the seas, he spent his life studying the creatures that lived in them. Cousteau made many wonderful films of his undersea adventures so everyone could see the amazing creatures that live in the ocean.

Cousteau worked to prevent ocean pollution and also invented the "aqua lung," a device that lets divers swim underwater for long periods of time. Today, many people enjoy underwater exploration with scuba equipment, based on Cousteau's invention.

★

3-D WOVEN FISH

You can make this woven fish as brightly colored as the most magnificent salt water fish, and show the fins in three-dimensions. Weave it in two or three colors, add fins, and hang it from the ceiling or glue to construction paper.

WHAT YOU NEED

Construction paper, 2 or 3 colors

Marker or crayon

Scissors

Tape

String

WHAT YOU DO

1 Fold a sheet of construction paper in half lengthwise. Draw one half of a fish on the fold of the paper, marking where all of the fins belong.

2 Cut out the fish. Make cuts along body for the fins and, as shown, for weaving.

3 Cut 3 or 4 strips, about 5" (12-13 cm) long and 1/2" (1 cm) wide, from different-colored construction paper.

4 Weave the strips in and out of the cuts in the fish's body to make a checkerboard pattern.

5 Draw a dorsal fin, anal fin, and ventral fins. Cut out, and stick them in the appropriate slits to create a 3-D effect.

6 Draw a curved line for gill slit. Then draw on an eye. Give your fish a big smile. Hang several fish from your ceiling with string, or paste or tape your fish onto construction paper.

HALF-A-FISH PATTERN

MAKE CUTS ON ALL DOTTED LINES

PLACE PATTERN ON PAPER FOLD

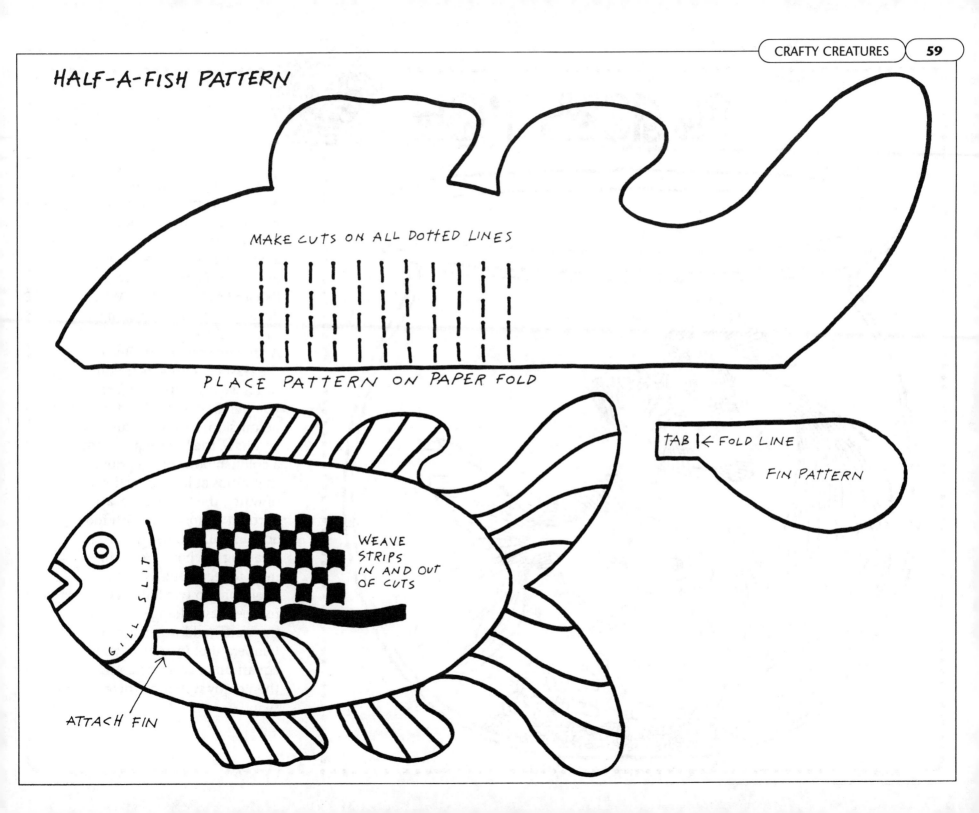

WEAVE
STRIPS
IN AND OUT
OF CUTS

GILL SLIT

ATTACH FIN

TAB ← FOLD LINE

FIN PATTERN

FLASHY FISH

MORE · SCIENCE · FUN!

Visit an aquarium if there is one in a city near you. You won't believe the fabulous fish you will get to see. Or, visit a pet store, and ask a lot of questions about fresh water fish and salt water fish. What do you notice from looking at the tanks?

A fish of your own: One of the least expensive pets you can have is goldfish. Before you purchase some, ask for permission, and make sure that you have the basic equipment: a goldfish bowl or aquarium that holds at least 10 gallons of water, the fish, fresh water at room temperature, fish food, and a small fish net when cleaning the bowl. You will need to feed your fish daily, about one to two flakes per fish per day. Change about half the water (add water at room temperature) in an unfiltered aquarium once a week. And then enjoy watching them swim!

SCIENCE TALK

A SCALY BUNCH

Alligators, crocodiles, turtles, and snakes all belong to a class of animals called *reptiles*. Reptiles are cold-blooded vertebrates, and most of them lay eggs. They breathe air and often crawl on their bellies like snakes or on short legs like lizards. They spend most of their time in and near the water. Their dry, scaly bodies work like armor to protect them. If they sound like any prehistoric animals you know, you are right! Dinosaurs were reptiles, too.

ALIKE AND DIFFERENT

Even though crocodiles and alligators look alike and are both reptiles, they are different, too. Crocodiles have pointed snouts, while alligators' snouts are more round. When an alligator's mouth is closed, its lower teeth are hidden by its upper teeth. But crocodiles have a notch at the side of their snout that exposes the long, fourth tooth on each side of their lower jaw.

Alligators and crocodiles are both well suited for watery life. Both reptiles have a kind of fleshy valve in their throat that keeps water out and lets them open their mouths in the water without choking. Also, their eyes are near the top of their heads, so they can submerge almost completely in water and still see what's going on above the surface. Both have feet that are webbed, which makes them better swimmers. And their nostrils, like their eyes, are almost on top of their heads, so they can breathe even when their bodies are almost completely underwater!

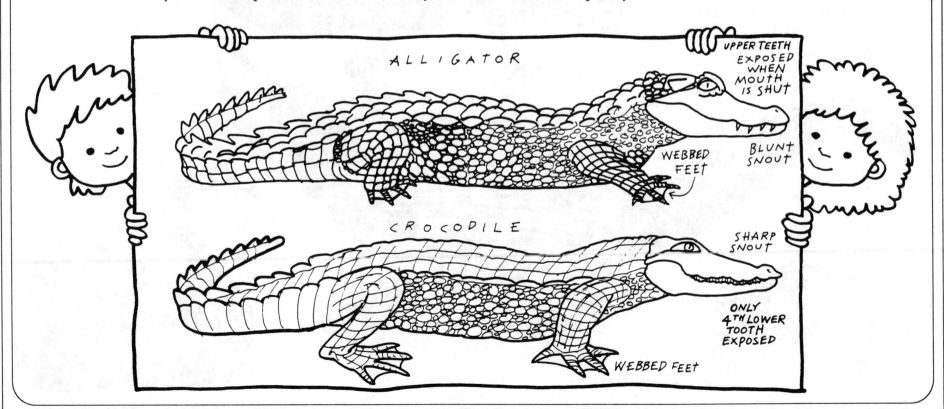

DETERMINED AND FAST

Many animals know that outrunning a determined crocodile can be hard work. Crocs, as they're sometimes called, have been known to crawl from the water and move on land at short bursts of speed — sometimes as fast as 15 to 30 miles (24 – 48 km) per hour! Next time you ride in a car with a grown-up, ask to go 30 miles per hour so you can feel how fast this is. Crocodiles aren't as fast when they're in the water — only 20 mph! (32.5 kmh) — but they can keep up a swimming chase for a longer period of time.

TURTLES

Turtles, some of the world's oldest reptiles, are found all over the world in many different shapes and sizes — as tiny as the 4½-inch (11–12 cm) bog turtle to the 7- to 8-foot-long (1.5 m) leatherback turtle that weighs as much as a car! All turtles are toothless omnivores that eat just about anything, living or dead. They cut their food with their beak and use strong throat muscles to push bite-size pieces down their throat.

Turtles are very well adapted to life in the wild. Their hard upper and lower shells are made of many connected bony plates that protect them from the fiercest of predators. A bridge connects the two shells so the turtle is secure.

Sadly, many turtles are in danger of extinction, in part, because they have been overhunted and also because their habitats are being destroyed by pollution or development.

For a clever look at turtle lore, read Aesop's famous fable, "The Tortoise and the Hare," and discover the meaning behind "Slow and steady wins the race."

MIGHTY MOLLUSKS

Most of us think of an octopus as a huge creature with eight long appendages spreading out from a central body. Actually most octopuses are only the size of your hand, but the biggest ones could stretch their appendages, called *tentacles*, all the way across your kitchen!

Octopuses belong to a phylum of animals called *mollusks* that have soft bodies; many mollusks have hard shells or shell-like coverings and live in the ocean near the shore. Are mollusks vertebrates or invertebrates? (If you said invertebrates, then you are absolutely right!)

How does an octopus feed itself? An octopus uses its tentacles with their suction cups along the underside to catch clams, crabs, lobsters, and other shellfish for eating. Pretty handy!

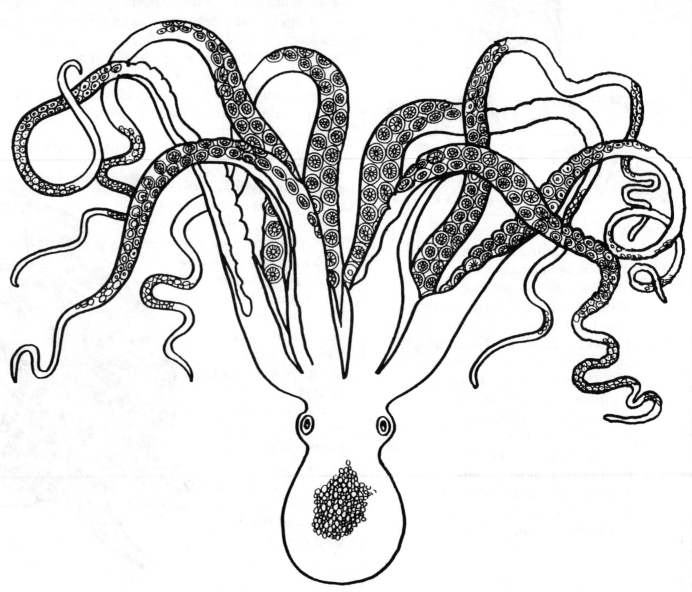

SCIENCE TALK

HIDDEN MEANINGS

You can figure out a lot about a word by the way it is spelled. "Octo" is a Latin word that means "eight," and octopus means "eight feet." There are many other words that begin with "oct," such as octagon. How many sides does an octagon have? Look in the dictionary to find other "oct"-words. But, don't be fooled by October. October used to be the eighth month of the year in the early Roman calendar, but in the calendar we use now (called the Gregorian calendar), it is actually the tenth month of the year!

STARTING OVER

AMAZING BUT TRUE

What happens if an octopus injures one of its tentacles? Well, you might think it would have to learn to manage with just seven, instead of eight. Believe it or not, an octopus can grow a new tentacle to replace an injured one. This process, called *regeneration*, means to create something again. Starfish are also able to regenerate cells and grow new limbs. In fact, most animals are able to regenerate in some way, although only simpler animals can regenerate whole body parts.

Animals' bodies are made of billions of cells, and many kinds of cells can renew themselves. Just think about the last time you cut yourself. Your wound healed eventually, didn't it? Wounds heal themselves by regenerating skin to cover it. So you see, regeneration is surely one of life's most wonderful gifts.

IN FOCUS

A MAGICAL METAMORPHOSIS

Do you know the Hans Christian Andersen story, *The Ugly Duckling*, about a duckling that grows up to be a lovely swan? Well, caterpillars make an even more amazing change, called *metamorphosis* (met uh MOR fuh sus), into that beautiful *insect*, the butterfly!

First, there is a tiny butterfly egg that hatches into a small caterpillar, or *larva*. Larvae love to eat and as a larva grows, it sometimes sheds its outgrown skin. At the right time, the caterpillar fastens itself to a leaf or twig with a sticky thread from inside its body. The caterpillar then spins a *cocoon*, or covering, around itself, in the *pupa* stage of its metamorphosis.

Big changes go on inside the cocoon; over a period of several days to six months, the pupa changes into a beautiful adult, now called a butterfly. When it emerges from the cocoon, the butterfly hangs in place until its wings and body are dry and firm, ready to begin its life as an adult.

PLEASED TO MEET YOU!

Luckily for all of us, butterflies are found just about anywhere in the world — and there are thousands of different kinds, too. The smallest butterflies are tinier than the end of your thumb, while the biggest have a wingspread as wide as a dinner plate!

A garden of colorful wings: If you want to get acquainted with some different species of butterflies, just plant marigolds, zinnias, cosmos, and nasturtiums — butterflies seem to love them! Throughout the summer, record how many different kinds of butterflies you observe by sketching in colored pencils or crayons what each one looks like. (Don't touch, of course.) Put the date and any unusual characteristics you notice next to each drawing.

Callaway Gardens in Pine Mountain, Georgia has an indoor garden, called a *conservatory*, that has over one thousand types of butterflies from around the world. Call your state Extension Service to see if there are any special butterfly gardens near you.

"STAINED-GLASS" BUTTERFLIES

Butterflies are so delicate you will only want to look at them — not touch or catch them. Their wings are covered with tiny overlapping scales that give them their lovely colors. Here's a way to make a butterfly image to brighten your bedroom window.

WHAT YOU NEED

Sheet of paper

Marker or crayon

Waxed paper

Tissue paper, many colors, cut in 1" (2.5 cm) squares

Liquid starch (spray, not aerosol)

Pipe cleaners

Tape

WHAT YOU DO

1 Draw a butterfly outline on the paper. Place a sheet of waxed paper on top so the outline shows through.

2 Spray plenty of starch on the waxed paper. Cover the butterfly shape with overlapping squares of tissue paper, in any design you like as long as you fill in the whole butterfly. Spray the waxed paper again with starch and add another layer of tissue squares.

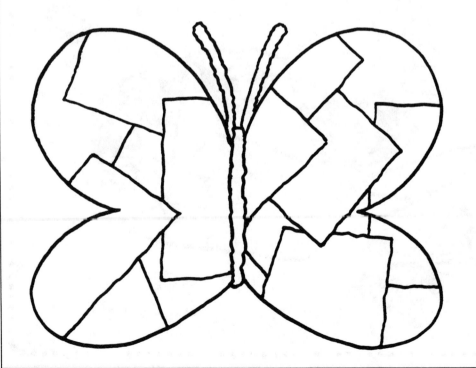

3 Add a third layer if you wish, finishing with another spray of starch. Throw away the paper outline; let the butterfly dry overnight. When dry, peel off the waxed paper very carefully.

4 To make the body, place a pipe cleaner along the line separating the left and right wings, bending the ends around the top and bottom, as shown. Tape in place.

5 Thread a second pipe cleaner through the top of the body, give it a twist, and bend the ends into a "V" for antennae. Hang in a sunny window.

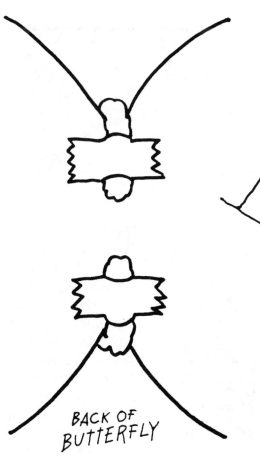

BACK OF BUTTERFLY

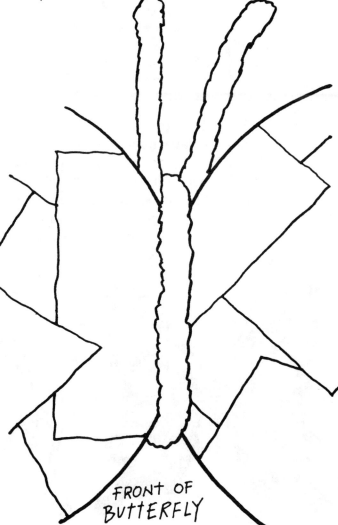

FRONT OF BUTTERFLY

THE BUTTERFLY AND THE BEETLE

It's hard to believe that a beautiful butterfly and a crawling beetle have much in common, but the fact is that they both belong to a class, named *insect*, of a phylum, named *arthropoda*, in the *animal* kingdom. Butterflies and beetles share the insect characteristics of three pairs of legs, bodies divided into three parts, and usually two pairs of wings. Insects are the most plentiful and widespread of all land animals.

A MATTER OF TASTE

Because butterflies can't bite or sting, they need other ways to protect themselves from predators. Some butterflies are very fast fliers. Others disguise, or *camouflage*, themselves to look just like dead leaves.

The North American monarch butterfly has a taste birds hate. The monarch's wings are very brightly colored, so birds know to stay away from them to avoid their awful taste. Another North American butterfly, the viceroy, looks almost like the monarch. Birds often mistake it for the monarch and don't eat it either, thinking it tastes terrible, too! Nature can be very clever in its adaptations for survival.

TOOL & TECHNIQUES

STEP INTO MY PARLOR

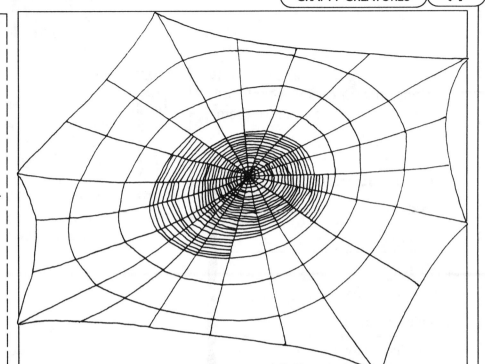

You may be surprised to know that spiders are *not* insects. While they do seem a lot alike and, like insects they belong to the phylum *arthropoda*, spiders belong to the class *Arachnida*, with eight, jointed legs and only two body sections, a head and abdomen, plus an *exoskeleton*, the hard, protective, covering outside the body. And if you see wings, you are not looking at a spider, because they don't have any.

If all this sounds like a description of one of your favorite seashore meals, you are absolutely right. Lobsters, shrimps, and crabs are also members of the arthropod phylum. See how classification helps sort things out!

STRONG AS STEEL

AMAZING BUT TRUE

Few things seem more fragile than a spider web in the glistening morning dew. Who would guess that pound for pound, a spider's silk is actually stronger than steel! Scientists discovered the silk's strength by testing its *tensile strength*, or the amount of stress it takes to make it tear. The strongest spider's silk has a tensile strength that's five times that of steel. Now that's pretty strong!

This super silk is made out of a liquid that comes out of tiny tubes called *spinnerets* at the rear of the spider's body. This liquid hardens into threads, some of which are sticky. When an insect flies into the web, it gets stuck there. As the insect tries to get loose, it shakes the threads of the web, sending the spider a message that dinner is waiting!

CLIMBING SPIDERS

Notice the eight legs and two body sections on your cardboard spider. Make a few climbers and race them up and down.

WHAT YOU NEED

Cardboard

Scissors

Tape

Crayons or markers

4 pipe cleaners

Drinking straw

String, 36" (90 cm) piece

WHAT YOU DO

1 Draw two circles on the cardboard, one 4" (10 cm) across and the other 2" (5 cm) across. Cut out the circles and tape them together on both sides, as shown. The bigger circle is the spider's abdomen; the smaller one is its head. Color in any design you wish.

2 Tape 4 pipe cleaners on the back of the head, just above where it joins the abdomen. Bend the legs in the middle so two pairs point forward and two point backward.

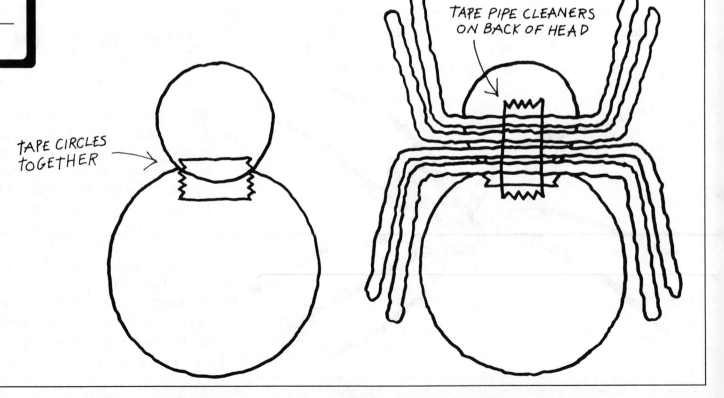

TAPE CIRCLES TOGETHER

TAPE PIPE CLEANERS ON BACK OF HEAD

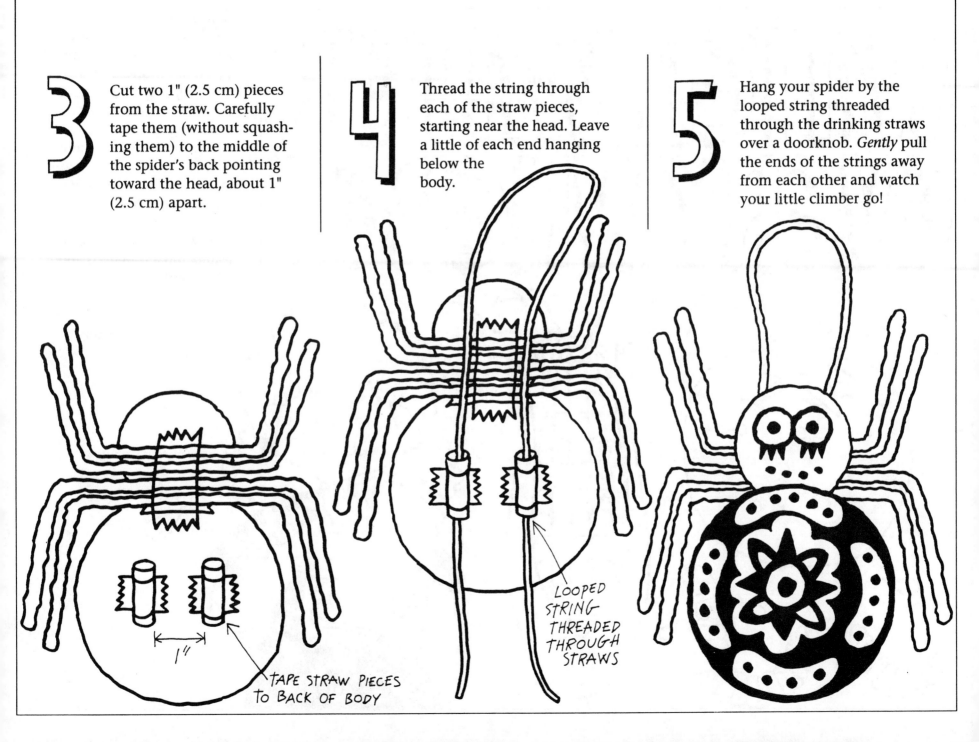

3 Cut two 1" (2.5 cm) pieces from the straw. Carefully tape them (without squashing them) to the middle of the spider's back pointing toward the head, about 1" (2.5 cm) apart.

4 Thread the string through each of the straw pieces, starting near the head. Leave a little of each end hanging below the body.

5 Hang your spider by the looped string threaded through the drinking straws over a doorknob. *Gently* pull the ends of the strings away from each other and watch your little climber go!

1"

TAPE STRAW PIECES TO BACK OF BODY

LOOPED STRING THREADED THROUGH STRAWS

WATER, WATER, EVERYWHERE

Water really is just about everywhere; in fact, it is the most common substance found on Earth, covering over 70 percent of the Earth's surface. It is in the air we breathe and in the ground we walk on — and it is in us, too! Our bodies are made up of about 65 percent water. An ear of corn is about 70 percent water; an earthworm about 80 percent water, and a tomato is about 95 percent water! Maybe instead of a bacon, lettuce, and tomato sandwich, you should ask for a bacon, lettuce, and water sandwich!

THREE IN ONE

Water is the only substance on Earth that comes in three different forms in normal temperature ranges — as the *liquid* water that you pour into a glass, as the solid ice that you can ice skate on in the winter, and as the gas water vapor that causes your tea kettle to whistle. Amazingly, if you change water from one form to another and back again, you will end up with the same amount of water that you started with. Actually, the total amount of water on the Earth and floating above the Earth as water vapor remains about the same at all times. There is about as much water today as there was hundreds of years ago — or ever will be!

Changing form: Measure a half cup of water and pour it into a small paper cup. Place the cup in the freezer for several hours. Once it is frozen, remove from the freezer, peel away the paper cup, and place the ice in the measuring cup. How much water is in the measuring cup after the ice melts? What are your conclusions about the changes that took place?

TAKING SHAPE

Place an apple in a dish. What shape does it have? (An apple shape, of course!) An apple holds its shape when you set it down. That makes an apple a *solid* object, because solids hold their shape no matter where you place them. Now, pour some water in a dish. What shape does it have? Water can't hold a shape of its own, can it? It is a *liquid*, and liquids always take the shape of the container they are in, as you can see right in your own kitchen.

WHAT YOU NEED

Water or juice

Plastic containers, in different shapes

Food coloring (optional)

WHAT YOU DO

1 Pour some water into a container. Add some food coloring for fun. Do you see how the water takes on the shape of the container?

2 Now, pour the water into another container with a different shape. What shape is the water now? Try pouring water into all sorts of weirdly shaped containers. Can you trick the water into holding its "own" shape by pouring it quickly or slowly?

IN FOCUS

BUT WHAT ABOUT...?

So liquids do take the shape of their containers, but you might wonder about nonliquids that seem to hold their containers' shapes, too. When you go to the beach, wet sand packs nicely into shaped containers for building sandcastles. Does that mean that sand is a liquid, too?

That's the kind of thinking that will make you a good scientist — observing change and asking questions about it. Look at the sand with a magnifying glass. You'll see that each individual grain of sand has its own shape. Even if you move the sand from one container to another, the grains still have their own individual shape. By adding the water, the grains of sand stick together just enough to hold the container's shape, but the individual grains of sand haven't changed shape, so they are solids, not liquids.

A WATCHFUL EYE!

Observing change is one of the skills of a good scientist, because the natural world is changing all the time. Some things change quickly, like the sun going behind a cloud. Some things change very, very slowly, like a rock being worn away by water into grains of sand over hundreds of years. Some change you can predict from what you already know, such as a puddle of water will turn to ice when the temperature falls below 32° F (0° C).

Keep a watchful eye out for things that change around you. Notice leaves, plants, wildlife, food, friends, and family. Do some things always seem to change in the same way? If so, what do you think *causes* the change? Can you begin to *predict* what will happen under certain conditions? Look everywhere in your life: If you stay up late, are you usually late for school? If no one waters the house-plants, do they start to droop?

FINDING YOUR WATER SOURCE

It is so easy to turn on a faucet and get some cold or hot water, we often forget that the water in our homes and schools is part of the water that must be shared by all living things on Earth. Depending on where you live, your water may come from a lake, a manmade reservoir, a mountain stream, a well, or a rain barrel. Ask a grown-up to explain where the water you drink is gathered and where it is *purified*, or

cleaned. Perhaps you can visit a water treatment plant that takes polluted water and purifies it so that it can be used for drinking and washing. It's hard to imagine, but on average, each person in the United States uses 70 gallons (260 liters) of water every day! What can you do to help *conserve*, or save, water? How about turning off the water in the sink while you brush your teeth for starters!

HERE COMES THE RAIN!

When you see clouds in the sky, you are actually seeing millions of water droplets in the form of gas vapor. Clouds form when warm, moist air above a body of water, such as a lake or ocean, rises in the air as water vapor. From there it meets cold air and forms into tiny little drops of water vapor we see as clouds. When the air gets too cold, the water vapor changes back into water drops (that is, from a gas back to a liquid), and falls back to the Earth as rain.

Try this experiment with a grown-up and create some rain right in your own kitchen!

WHAT YOU NEED

2 saucepans

1 cup (250 ml) water

Ice cubes

Potholders

WHAT YOU DO

1 Ask a grown-up to help you heat a cup of water in a saucepan, but do not let it come to a boil.

2 Put ice cubes in the other saucepan, and hold above the hot water. Be sure to use potholders.

3 Watch for small drops of water to form on the bottom of the ice cube pan. The water vapor from the saucepan on the stove *condenses*, changing into water drops when it hits the cold saucepan with the ice in it.

...BUT NOT A DROP TO DRINK!

If 70 percent of the Earth is covered with water, and if the amount of water on Earth and in the air always stays the same, why do we have water shortages and not enough water to drink?

Only 3 percent of the water on Earth is really available to us to drink. The oceans hold 97 percent of the water on Earth, and of course, that water is salty. (When salt water evaporates though, most of the salt is left behind and the water that falls as rain is fresh water.) Huge glaciers hold most of the fresh water, and that is not available to us as drinking water either.

Be a good scientist and make a list of what changes are taking place that might cause water shortages. Here are some things you might include in your list:

1 **Weather patterns:** Maybe it hasn't rained as much as usual.

2 **Population:** Have a lot of people moved to an area?

3 **Industry:** Is there a large, new manufacturing plant that uses water in the area?

4 **Environment:** Was there a major storm or construction resulting in erosion that caused water to run off into the rivers instead of soaking into the ground? Have a lot of forests been cut down?

5 **Contamination:** Is something poisonous, or *toxic*, leaking into the rivers and lakes, making the water unusable by humans and other animals?

What other observations can you make that might explain water shortages?

SCIENCE TALK

WHAT IS ACID RAIN?

Water is naturally clean enough to drink, but because of pollution from automobile exhaust, volcanoes and big industrial plants, more and more rain water is reaching the Earth already contaminated with toxins. You see, when harmful pollutants in the atmosphere mix with moisture, they create a terrible mixture called acid rain. Every year, acid rain and acid snow kill plants, hurt animal life, and pollute drinking water.

Acid rain doesn't only fall near the factories or heavy traffic. Strong winds carry the pollution in the air to parts of the world that are otherwise clean, causing acid rain there, too.

To help stop acid rain, ask your family and friends to share car rides or take buses to limit the number of cars on the road.

SAVE THE RAINFORESTS

Rainforests are one of nature's amazing ways of taking care of itself. Many places on Earth rely on tropical rainforests for clean air and rainwater. That's because these special forests, found near the equator, are thick with trees and plants that soak up large amounts of rain. Then, they release water vapor, through a process called *transpiration*, and oxygen, through *photosynthesis*, back into the air, making clouds and clean air. The clouds sometimes travel thousands of miles releasing water in the form of rain in places where it would otherwise be dry!

What you can do: Explain to some friends or to your classmates why it is so important to save the rainforests. Remember that all living things need water and clean air. If you want to learn more about the rainforests or do more to save them, write to these organizations for free information:

Rainforest Alliance
270 Lafayette St., Suite 512
New York, NY 10012
(212) 677-1900

Rainforest Action Network
301 Broadway, Suite A
San Francisco, CA 94133
(415) 398-4404

NATURE'S ART

NATURAL WONDERS

Nature has a wonderful way of creating its own artistic masterpieces — just think of snowflakes! Snowflakes form when water vapor in the air condenses (turns from vapor to water) around a frozen drop of water called a *crystal*. Many small crystals of frozen water attach to each other making snowflakes. Snowflakes are hexagonal, or six-sided, but that doesn't mean they all look the same.

For snow to fall, the temperature has to be below the freezing point (32° F or 0° C). **Snowflake art:** If you live where it snows, you'll want to look closely at some snowflakes. When it first starts to snow big flakes, take a magnifying glass and a piece of dark construction paper outdoors. With the magnifying glass, look closely at the individual flakes that land on the paper. They're amazing, aren't they? Each flake is perfectly formed and is different from every other flake. Go inside, make some hot cocoa, and draw some snow-flakes in your lab book or write a poem about nature's art.

"SNOWFLAKE" BENTLEY

❄

Have you ever heard someone say that "no two snowflakes are alike"? Well, thanks to Wilson Bentley, a farmer and scientist from Vermont, we know this is true! "Snowflake" Bentley, as he was often called, spent every spare moment of his life studying and photographing — you guessed it — snowflakes. His curiosity about snow led him to take more than 5800 photos of snowflakes!

Bentley was a man whose ideas were way ahead of his time; even brilliant scientists didn't understand his work at first. Yet Bentley never once let other people's opinions stop him from doing his work. If you'd like to see Snowflake Bentley's marvelous photographs, take a look at his book *Snow Crystals*. Maybe you'll be inspired to draw or take pictures of the natural world around you.

❄

STAYING AFLOAT

Have you ever wondered why you can float when you are stretched out on your back in a lake or pool (never go in water without a grown-up watching, of course), but if you scrunch into a ball you sink? Well, it has to do with how much water is pushing against you and how much muscle mass is in your body. When you stretch out more water pushes against you; when you scrunch up, less water is pushing against you. Here's a way to see this scientific principle in action — right in your kitchen sink.

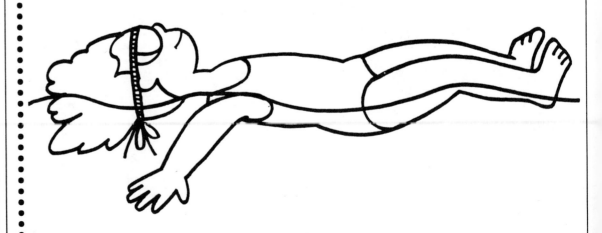

WHAT YOU NEED

Sink full of water

2 pieces of clay

WHAT YOU DO

1 Scrunch one piece of clay into a small, tight ball. Shape the other piece into a flat-bottomed boat.

2 Before you put the clay into the water, *predict* which piece — if any — will float. The ball? The boat? Both? Neither?

3 Now place both the ball and the boat in the water. What happens? Can you explain why?

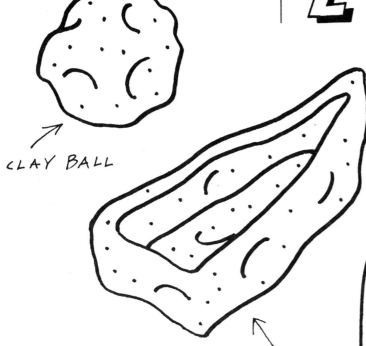

CLAY BALL

CLAY BOAT

 TECHNIQUES & TOOLS

PREDICTIONS AND CONCLUSIONS

In science, the more carefully you look around and listen, the more you will begin to understand what is happening around you. Soon, you will find you can make an "educated guess," or *prediction*, about what is going to happen. Predictions are made before you experiment, and they are based on what you already know, just like a hypothesis is (see page 16). If you understood that things are more likely to float if they are spread out, you might have predicted that the boat would float, and the ball would sink.

Conclusions, on the other hand, are based on what you learn from your procedure, results, and observations. You might conclude that the foil ball sank to the bottom because it was squeezed into a small shape, and therefore only a small amount of water was pushing against it to hold it up.

Prediction and conclusion are two very important parts of scientific thinking.

THEY JUST DON'T MIX

 SCIENCE TALK

Did you ever notice what happens to salad dressing made with oil and water? They don't stay mixed together even after you shake them. When two liquids separate themselves into layers, like oil and water do, we say the two liquids are *immiscible* (ih MISS ih buhl).

Science is all around us. Understanding immiscible liquids helps us understand the world around us. We can use *observation* and *prediction*, and *cause* and *effect* to understand why an oil spill on a lake or ocean is so damaging. We can understand why it doesn't help to pour water on a fire that involves greasy (oily) foods in the kitchen. And if we ever wondered how wild animals, like beavers and otters, live in icy cold water, we only have to observe their oily fur coats that help repel water away from their skin.

LAYERED LIQUIDS

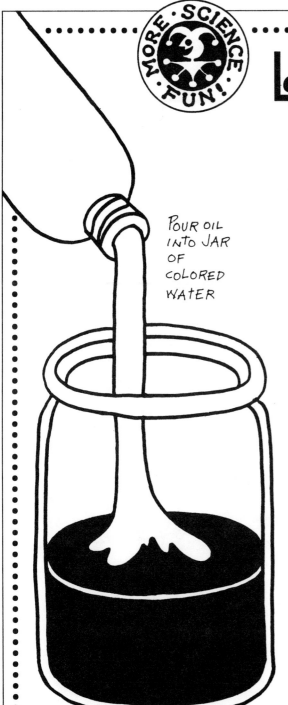

POUR OIL INTO JAR OF COLORED WATER

After a rainstorm, you might notice puddles in the road with glossy-looking oil floating on top. Why does the oil float on water? See what conclusions you can draw from this experiment.

WHAT YOU NEED

Glass jars (2)
Food coloring
Water
Vegetable oil
Rubbing alcohol

WHAT YOU DO

1 Put a drop of food coloring into a jar of water; then pour some vegetable oil on top. (The food coloring is added so you can see the layers more clearly; it doesn't change the outcome of the experiment.)

2 What happens? Now, stir or shake the jar. Do the oil and water stay mixed?

3 Take another jar of colored water. Pour some rubbing alcohol slowly down the side of the jar. Stir or shake. Do the liquids stay mixed?

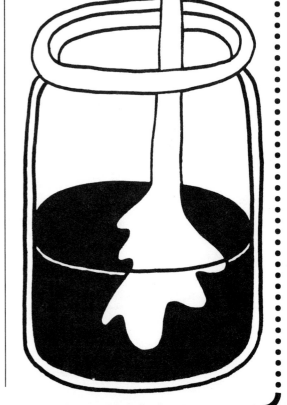

POUR COLORED RUBBING ALCOHOL SLOWLY DOWN SIDE OF JAR INTO WATER

PRETTY PAPER

Knowing that oil floats on water can also help you explain why this method of making beautiful marbleized paper works.

WHAT YOU NEED

Shallow baking dish

Water

Oil-based paint (2 or 3 colors)

Stirring stick or twig

Paper

Paper towels

Hand-cleaning gel or turpentine

WHAT YOU DO

1 Cover your work area with newspaper and wear an old shirt. Fill the baking dish almost to the top with water.

2 Dip a stirring stick into one of the paints and drip the paint in a swirling pattern over the water. Wipe the stick with a paper towel and do the same with another color. Use a third color if you like, but more than three might start to look muddy.

3 Put a sheet of paper right onto the surface of the water in the pan. Lift it off immediately and lay it, paint-side-up, on newspaper. Your paper will be covered with a colored, swirly design that looks like a slab of marble.

4 To clean up, use paper towels to soak up the paint. Then, pour off the water and the pan should clean up easily.

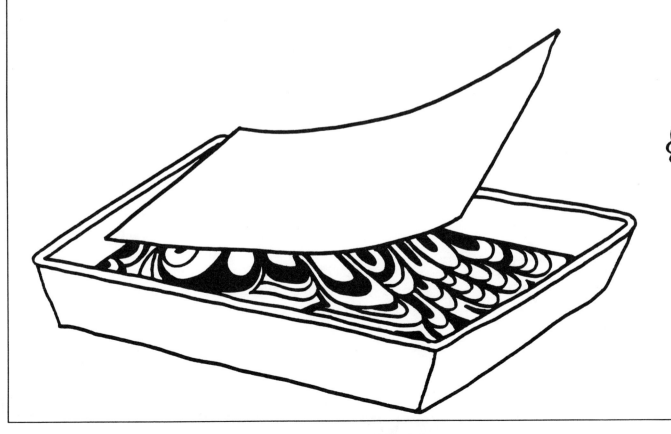

THE AIR AROUND US

Can you answer this science riddle?

You can't see me,
You can't hold onto me,
You can pass through me;
I take up space, even though
I have no shape of my own.
What am I?

If you guessed water, you are almost correct, except you can see water, and when it is in its solid form, you can hold it as a freezing cold ice cube. So what else could our riddle be describing? Did you guess air? Air is something we can't see, we can't hold onto, yet it's almost everywhere! In fact, since we can't see, smell, taste, or touch air, we really know about air because of the things it does. Did you ever think that because of air we can

● drink a glass of milk through a straw,
● blow up a balloon so it is big and round,
● see air bubbles underwater, or watch soap bubbles float toward the sky,
● feel moving air, called *wind*, blow our hair.

Air does all of this, and lots more, too. So what exactly is air? Air, or the *atmosphere* as it is sometimes called, is a mixture of gases; actually 78 percent of the air is nitrogen and 21 percent is oxygen, with only one percent other gases. Floating in the gases are water droplets, ice crystals, and fine dust particles, but these are not considered part of the air. This invisible mixture is so important, we couldn't live without it!

THE STUFF OF LIFE

All living things need air to live. People have survived as long as a month without food and more than a week without water, but a human being can only live a few minutes without air!

As if that is not enough, air does a whole lot more for all of us creatures on Earth.

➤ Air traps the warmth of the sun near the Earth, keeping the Earth warm enough to support plant and animal life.

➤ The movement of air and the water vapor in the air help form clouds that bring us the rainwater we need in order to live.

➤ Air helps us hear because the soundwaves travel through air.

It sure is a lot easier to understand and believe what you can see, so how do you think a good scientist goes about studying something that is invisible like air? You must strengthen your *powers of observation*, looking more closely at actions and reactions, sometimes called *causes and effects*. "If I do this, then that happens." What action was the cause, and what reaction was the effect or result?

The other thing every good scientist does is to ask lots of questions about what is observed. If you notice bubbles underwater, what is causing them? Why do they float to the surface? Can you make more bubbles or cause them to stop forming?

And one more thought: There is no such thing as a bad question. If a question brings you closer to understanding something, then that is all that really matters. So ask away!

"Seeing" air: It is possible to "see" air — well, sort of. Next time you're in the bathtub, push a paper cup straight down under the water so it is open-side down against the tub's bottom. Then tip the cup's edge and watch what happens. Almost magically, bubbles rise toward the surface. So what are the bubbles made of? AIR! The air was trapped in the cup, and when you tilted it, some of the air escaped to the surface, and water rushed in to take the place of the escaping air.

SEEING IS BELIEVING

GIANT FLOATING BUBBLES

Bubbles are air or gas trapped inside a liquid ball. To make long-lasting bubbles be sure that everything that comes into contact with them is wet, preferably with the bubble-making solution.

WHAT YOU NEED

Basin or dish pan

4 cups (1 l) water

2 cups (500 ml) liquid dish detergent

2 cups (500 ml) glycerine (available in most drug stores)

2 teaspoons (10 ml) corn syrup

Wire hangers

WHAT YOU DO

1 Mix the water, detergent, glycerin, and corn syrup in a large basin or dish pan.

2 Bend a wire hanger into a circle, a star, or other interesting closed shape.

3 Submerge your hanger in the basin, and lift it out gently. Now hold it carefully — and run! Watch the bubbles blow behind you.

WEIGHING IN!

IN FOCUS

How would you prove that air has weight, if you can't see it, taste it, smell it, or hold it? This is where a very good strategy for all of your learning comes in: *Go to what you know.* Whether you are solving a math problem, developing a science experiment, or trying to spell a new word, if you start with what you know and then build on that one step at a time, you will reach some new ideas and conclusions. It works every time.

Let's see how "go to what you know" works in proving that air has weight. Start with the obvious. How would you weigh a solid like an orange? (That's simple; place it on a scale and read what it weighs.)

How would you weigh a liquid like water? Well, you might think to yourself, water needs to be in a container to hold it, so you would pour the water in a jar and weigh it, but then you have the weight of the water and the jar. Better to first weigh the jar alone, then weigh the jar with the water. Subtract the weight of the jar alone and you will have the weight of the water. That makes good sense.

So how would you prove that air has weight? Go to what you know. First you might remove all the air from a bottle with a small vacuum pump. Seal the airless (empty) bottle and weigh it. Then remove the seal, letting the bottle fill with air. Now weigh the air-filled bottle. It weighs more, proving that air, indeed, does weigh something!

FEELING THE PRESSURE

SCIENCE TALK

Since air has weight, it is held to the Earth by the force of gravity, just as you are. Since gravity is strongest near the Earth's surface, it holds most of the air, or atmosphere close to the Earth's surface. This pushing force of the air is called *air pressure*, and the closer to the Earth you are, the stronger the air pressure. The higher the altitude, the less the air pressure.

Ye olde straw experiment: Talk to anyone interested in science and chances are they will remember how the drinking straw experiment demonstrates how air pressure works right in your kitchen. Put a straw in a glass of water. Now suck some water up into the straw. Quickly cover the top of the straw with your finger. Lift the straw out of the glass. What happens? Nothing! No air can get into the top to allow the water to come out. Lift your finger. Now air can get into the top of the straw, and the water can flow out because of gravity.

MAGIC WATERING CAN

What makes this "magic" watering can work?

WHAT YOU NEED

Small container with plastic lid

Hammer and nail
(for grown-up use only)

Water

Colorful markers or other decorating materials

WHAT YOU DO

1 Ask a grown-up to help you punch 3 small holes in the bottom of the container with a hammer and nail. Punch one hole in the center of the plastic lid.

2 Decorate your container with waterproof markers, stickers, or scraps of contact paper cut into interesting shapes.

3 Fill your container partially with water and put on the lid. Some water will sprinkle out through the holes in the bottom. When you place your thumb firmly over the hole in the lid and press down, a stronger stream of water will come out.

4 *Gradually ease up on the pressure, keeping your thumb over the hole.* The water will stop completely! Now you can start and stop the flow of water by increasing and decreasing the pressure on the hole.

PUNCH A HOLE IN PLASTIC LID THEN PLACE ON OPEN END OF CONTAINER

PUNCH 3 HOLES IN BOTTOM OF CONTAINER

HOW'D THAT HAPPEN?

NATURAL WONDERS

So what's the scientific explanation for the magic watering can? Think about what you already know about air pressure and gravity from "ye olde straw experiment." The watering can is just a larger version of the single drinking straw. Even though the container is partially filled with water, there is air inside, too. When you press down on the lid, you also press down on the air. Since the air can't get out (there is water beneath it), it presses down on the water, forcing the water out of the holes in the bottom. When you stop pressing down but keep your finger over the opening, the pressure of the air *outside* the container holds the water *up* from the bottom, just like in the straw! What happens if you take the lid off completely? Now, air can enter the space above the water, and the water can flow out due to gravity.

AIR POWER

SCIENCE TALK

Wind results from the different temperatures of the air. Warm air rises, and colder air rushes in to take its place. That rushing colder air is what we call *wind*! You know wind can move things because of the way your hair blows in your face or the way flags flutter on a windy day. A good breeze can move a big sailboat or even a giant windmill. In fact, if you are on a high floor in a very tall building, you can feel the whole building sway back and forth in a strong wind.

MORE SCIENCE FUN!

Hot air is less dense than cool air, so hot air rises (like smoke coming out of a chimney), causing cooler air that is more dense to sink. If that cooler air is warmed up, then it will rise, replacing the now cooled-off air, and thus you will have a cycle of movement of air called a *convection cell*.

It's this air movement that causes all sorts of things to happen in the atmosphere, including winds to blow and clouds to form, move, and bring rain to dry areas. On a smaller scale, you can observe the effects of hot air rising, causing your hot-air-powered mobile to spin. Ask a grown-up to help you hang this safely above a lamp in your room.

WHAT YOU NEED

Round jar base to trace

Scraps of construction paper, different colors

Scissors

Thread

Paper clips

Dowel or hanger

WHAT YOU DO

1 Use the bottom of a glass or jar to draw a circle on a sheet of paper. Make the circle about 4" (10 cm) across, or make different sizes. Cut out.

2 Fold the circle in half. Then fold the semi-circle in half again. Now, fold the quarter circle in half again.

3 When you open your paper circle, it will be divided into 8 equal sections. On each fold line, make a dot about 1/2" (1 cm) from the outside of the circle. Cut each fold line just up to the dot.

4 Fold down one corner of each of the 8 sections.

5 Tie a thread about 12" long (30 cm) to the end of a paper clip. Poke a hole in the center of your spinner where the 8 fold-lines meet. (Vary thread lengths for a mobile.)

A HOT-AIR-POWERED MOBILE

6 Thread the free end through the hole so the paper clip hangs down from the middle, and the folded corners of the spinner point *down*. To make a spinner that moves in the opposite direction, fold the corners down in the opposite direction.

7 Attach your threads to a hanger, a stick, or a dowel. Hold over a lighted bulb of a lamp. (Ask for grown-up help. The bulb is hot enough to burn you so please do not touch!) Wait just a few seconds, and watch the spin begin!

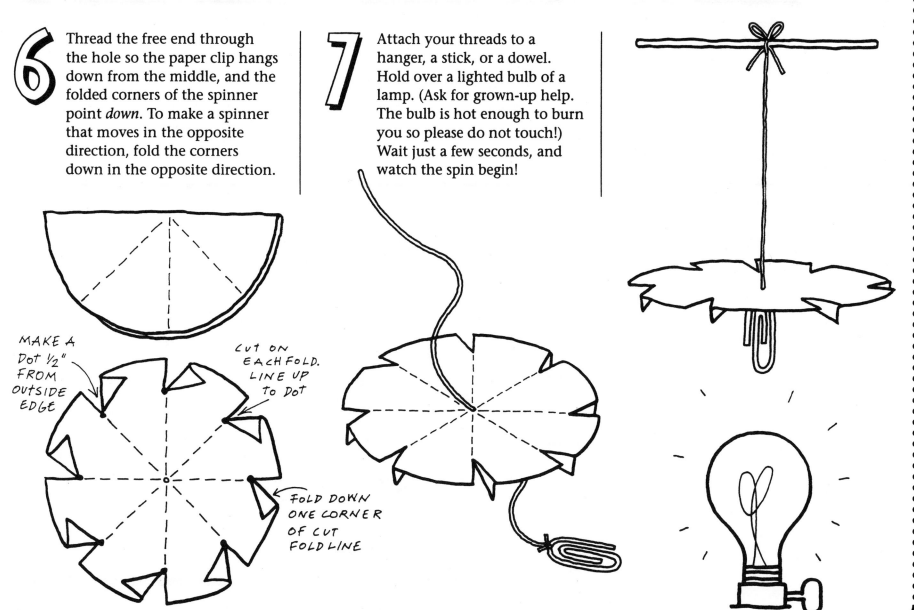

MAKE A DOT ½" FROM OUTSIDE EDGE

CUT ON EACH FOLD. LINE UP TO DOT

FOLD DOWN ONE CORNER OF CUT FOLD LINE

NATURAL WONDERS

A SEA BREEZE

Did you ever go to the beach on a really hot day? At home, people were probably saying things like, "It's so hot, there is not a breath of fresh air today," or "The air is sure still today." Off to the beach and what do you feel, a gentle breeze coming off the water. Can you go to what you know and *hypothesize*, or make an educated guess, as to why there is a breeze at the beach?

The beach absorbs heat faster than the water in the huge ocean. This causes the air above the beach to be warmer than the air above the ocean. The warmer air over the beach rises and the cooler air over the sea moves in, producing a delightful sea breeze. Mmmm, time to take a dip!

WINDMILLS ON MY MIND

If possible, ask a grown-up or your teacher or scout leader to take you to see a working windmill. You might find them on farms, powering an irrigation system. Windmills are beautiful to watch. They show how clever humans are in using their imaginations and science to help humankind without harming the environment.

Make your own handheld windmill (otherwise known as a pinwheel) to see the wind in action and to have some fun, too.

WHAT YOU NEED

Two different-colored scraps construction paper

Ruler

Scissors

Paste or glue

Thumbtack

Pencil with eraser

WHAT YOU DO

1 Cut out two 6" (15 cm) squares of construction paper. Lay one square exactly on top of the other.

2 Fold the squares so they form a triangle. Then fold the triangle in half to make a smaller triangle.

3 Open your squares to see two fold lines crisscrossing in the center. With the ruler, mark about 1" (2.5 cm) from the center on each fold line.

4 With scissors, cut on each fold line, stopping at the mark. Now you have four triangular sections, joined together at the center.

5 Holding the point of one section, bend it over so it touches the center. Hold it in place with a little dab of paste. Repeat so that one point of each section is pasted to the center.

6 Carefully stick a thumbtack through the center of the pinwheel, into the eraser of a pencil. The pinwheel should be attached firmly, but just enough to allow it to spin freely when you blow on it, or take it outdoors into a gentle wind.

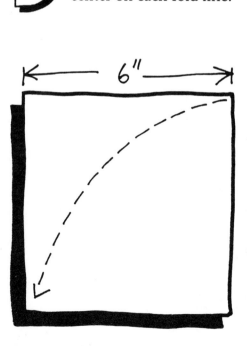

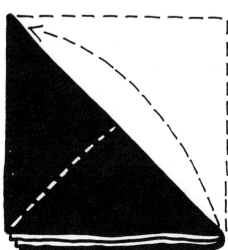

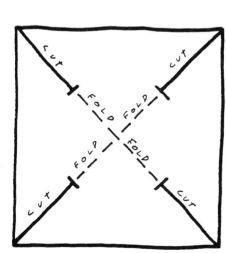

THE SKY ABOVE

As you may have noticed in the section on air, it is difficult to understand what you can't see. People have always tried to make sense of their world by telling stories such as Greek myths, medieval fables, and folktales.

Thus it went with humankind's explanation of the Earth below and the sky above. For many, many hundreds of years, the people of Earth thought that their world was flat. They believed if you got too close to its edge, you'd fall right off! It appeared to them that the sun, moon, and stars moved across the sky, so they assumed that these heavenly bodies moved around Earth, which stood still at the center of the universe.

The ancient Greeks and Romans believed the Earth was carried on the shoulders of a giant, named Atlas. The Chinese originally believed the Earth sat on the back of an enormous turtle.

Today we know the Earth is a huge, ball-shaped planet that moves *around* the sun. And no one has ever fallen off its edge, of course, because it's round!

SIZING THINGS UP

TECHNIQUES & TOOLS

The solar system refers to the nine planets that revolve around the sun. Earth is one of those nine planets — the third closest to the sun.

If you were to travel from the Earth to the sun, it would be an incredible journey — nearly 92,956,600 miles (149,598,000 kilometers) long! Pretty hard to imagine how far away that is, and harder still to comprehend how much farther away the planet Saturn is at 888,184,000 miles (1,427,010,000 kilometers) from the sun.

Far, farther, farthest: Giving meaning to huge numbers is done by figuring out a relationship or *ratio*, and then drawing everything *to scale*. For example, if your best friend lives 10 miles from you, your grandmother is 20 miles away, and your brother has a job in a town 30 miles away, you might develop a ratio where one inch equals 10 miles. To help you see or *visualize* their relative distances from you, you could draw a square on paper for your house; then draw a one-inch line for the distance to your friend's, and then a two-inch line and a three-inch line. All of a sudden it is very easy to see how these distances compare with each other. Figuring out ratios and drawing to scale let's us "see" numbers and distances that are too big or too small for us to imagine.

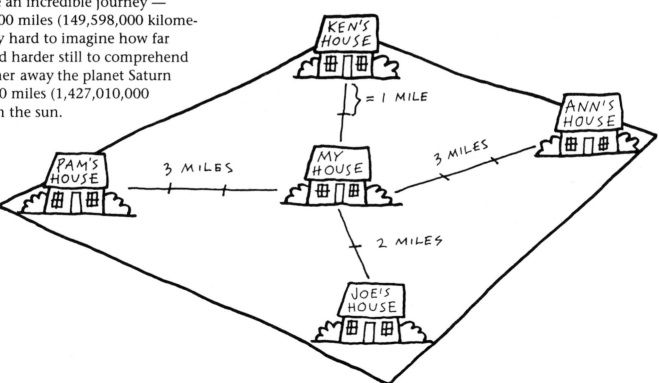

A SOLAR SYSTEM SUPPER

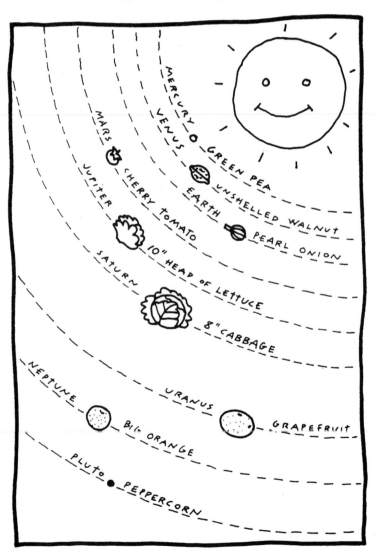

Invite your friends or surprise your family with a solar system supper. Make a tablecloth out of a long piece of brown butcher paper, draw a brightly colored sun at one end of the paper, and then draw each planet the distance from the sun to scale. Color each planet as suggested in the chart below (these are the colors of the planets as they appear through powerful telescopes). This scale of relative distances is based on the distance from the Earth to the sun equalling one inch.

MORE · SCIENCE · FUN!

Planet	Distance from Sun		Color	Size
Mercury	2/5"	(1 cm)	Orange	green pea
Venus	3/4"	(1.88 cm)	Yellow	unshelled walnut
Earth	1"	(2.5 cm)	Blue, brown, green	pearl onion
Mars	1½"	(3.75 cm)	Red	cherry tomato
Jupiter	5⅕"	(13 cm)	Yellow, red, brown	10" head of lettuce
Saturn	9½"	(23.75 cm)	Yellow	8" cabbage
Uranus	19⅕"	(48 cm)	Green	grapefruit
Neptune	30"	(75 cm)	Blue	big orange
Pluto	39²/₅"	(98.5 cm)	Yellow	peppercorn

Don't know how big to make each planet? A great way to gauge the relative sizes of the planets is to use the foods listed under "size" (adapted from Avery Hart and Paul Mantell in their book, *Kids and Weekends: Creative Ways to Make Special Days*). Draw your planets to these relative sizes and then make a salad for your supper with these "solar" ingredients. (The sun is too big to put into this salad! If you put it into this scale, it would be as big as a large house!) What else to put on your Solar System Supper menu? How about some "Planet Burgers" (burgers stuffed with a surprise chunk of "sun" cheese in the center) and an "Eclipse Sundae" (scoop of ice cream darkened with hot fudge).

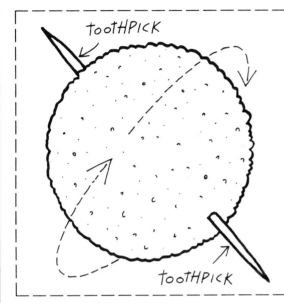

toothpick

toothpick

PICTURE THIS!

Have you ever heard the expression, "A picture is worth a thousand words"? Well, here's proof.

The Earth is a *sphere*, or rounded shape, that spins on an imaginary line called an axis. Take an orange and stick a toothpick in the top and another in the bottom. Hold the toothpicks at a slant, turn them slowly, and there you have it — the Earth (orange) on its *axis* (toothpicks).

That's called making a *model*, and it is a good science technique to help you visualize, or see, whatever it is you are trying to understand. Some models might be made to scale so you could see a relationship in size or distance, but in this case, you wanted a simple model that would help you see how the Earth and its axis function. The model explains it better than even a thousand words!

THE NINE OF US

SCIENCE TALK

Imagine if you had eight sisters and brothers, making nine kids in your family. Then, think what it would be like if you lived millions of miles away from each other. You and your sisters and brothers would develop very differently, and most likely have very little in common.

That's true of the nine planets. Though they all revolve around the sun, they have very little else in common. As far as we know, only the planet Earth has any life on it, although for years, scientists have been trying to prove that there is life on Mars.

Mercury is the closest planet to the sun, and as you might expect, being closest to the sun means being the hottest planet, too. In some places on Mercury, it's 800° F (427° C) — that's eight times hotter than the hottest place on Earth! Pluto is the coldest planet because — you guessed it — it's the farthest away from the sun!

Many people think of Venus as the Earth's twin, but life on Venus would be a lot different from our life on Earth. In fact, we could never live there because its atmosphere is filled with poisonous gases.

DAY AND NIGHT

The Earth's axis on one end is called the North Pole, while the other end is called the South Pole. The Earth is also slightly tilted, so when it spins on its axis, it looks much like a slanted top spinning on the floor. As the Earth rotates, one side faces toward the sun, providing that side of Earth with daylight. But as the Earth continues to rotate, that same side moves into darkness (now facing away from the sun), giving that part of the Earth nighttime. One complete turn of the earth on its axis equals 24 hours, a full day and night.

Who's moving?: Pick a favorite tree that grows away from tall buildings. Draw it first thing in the morning, labeling the time of day. Be sure to show exactly where the sunlight hits the tree, where the shadows are, and where the sun is in the sky. Visit the tree every four hours and draw it each time *from the exact same place,* observing the light, shadows, and position of the sun. What do you notice? Do the sun's rays hit the tree in the same place all day long? The rays appear to move around the tree, casting a shadow as they go. But it's not the sun that's moving in the sky, of course. It's the Earth!

A DIZZYING RIDDLE

AMAZING-BUT-TRUE

What moves while it stands still?

Here's a hint for you: The earth rotates on its axis every 24 hours. And, the Earth is about 25,000 miles (40,000 km) around its widest part, the equator. So what's the answer to the riddle? You are! Even though you feel like you are standing still, you'd be moving at about 1,000 miles (1600 km) per hour if you were standing at the equator; otherwise, not quite as fast, though plenty fast enough! (Divide miles or km by 24.) Feeling dizzy?

So day and night happen in 24 hours because the Earth spins on its axis. But that's not all the spinning you are doing. As the Earth rotates on its axis every 24 hours, it also moves around the sun making a complete *orbit*, or trip, every 365 days. That's right, the Earth and its relationship with the sun not only controls day and night, it also controls the four seasons of the year!

Act it out!: Place an object on the floor. That's the sun. You can be the Earth. Now walk around the "sun" in a wide circle, and also spin slowly as you walk. Do you see how the Earth both rotates on its axis and also revolves, or turns, around the sun at the same time?

ROUND AND ROUND WE GO

SCIENCE TALK

SUN TALES

IN FOCUS

There's a folktale from the Jicarilla Apache of southwest North America, explaining how the sun got up in the sky. They tell of a boy, named Holy Boy, who stole a small object known to be the sun from an enemy named White Hacticin. Holy Boy placed the sun in the sky for the rest of his people to admire and respect, and that is how the sun came to be in the sky.

If you were to create a story about the sun, what would it say? In a way, folktales used a basic principle of science, the power of observation. People used what they saw and combined it with what they felt, to explain the unknown. Make up your own Sun Tales and share them with a friend — on a sunny day, of course!

MORE · SCIENCE · FUN!

Long before clocks were invented, people used sundials as their first time-telling machines. When the sun moved across the sky, the shadow on a sundial moved from point to point in the same way. See for yourself how this works. Shine a flashlight on a tall object from one side and see where the object casts its shadow. Now, while you shine the light on the object, walk around it. As you move the light, does the shadow move, too?

WHAT YOU NEED

Modeling clay

Bowl

Drinking straw

Construction paper

Scissors, tape, pencil

SUN CLOCKS

WHAT YOU DO

1 Roll out a lump of clay into a round, flat shape. Place a bowl over the flat clay and trim the clay around the edges.

2 Cut out a paper sun design, larger than your clay circle. Place the clay in the center of your paper.

3 Curl a piece of paper into a cone shape, 1" (2.5 cm) long. Tape the ends together so the bottom is even all around.

4 Stick the straw into the middle of the clay so it stands up straight. Hang the cone upside down over the top of the straw.

Using your sundial: Take your sundial outside early on a sunny day, and place it where the sun will hit it all day long. Every hour on the hour that the sun is out — 8:00 AM, 9:00 AM, 10:00 AM, and so on — make a groove in the clay with a pencil along the shadow of the straw and write the hour in the clay. Once you've marked off all the daylight hours on the clay, your sundial will always give you the time *at this spot* — at least when the sun is shining!

If you move the sundial, you need to place it correctly when you take it back outside. Make a small mark on the edge of the dial that you can line up with another mark that you make on the ground. Want a permanent sundial? Just use materials for your sundial that won't be damaged by rain.

THE FOUR SEASONS

NATURAL WONDERS

If you love to swim in the summer and play in the snow in the winter, then you are sure to be fascinated by the seasons. There are two major reasons why we have different seasons and you already know about both of them. So let's see how they work together.

It takes slightly more than 365 days for the Earth in its path, or *orbit*, to move completely around the sun. The Earth is always *tilted* on its axis at an angle of 23.5°. When the tilt is closest to the sun, the northern hemisphere, or top half of the Earth, has summer. As the Earth travels around the sun, the same tilt gradually faces away from the sun and the northern hemisphere has winter while the southern hemisphere enjoys summer (because now it is receiving more direct rays from the sun). The two hemispheres are always enjoying the opposite seasons.

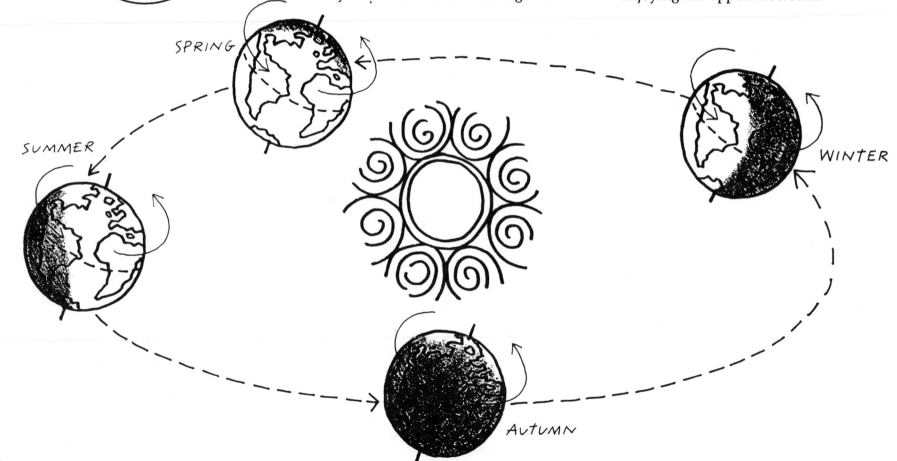

SPRING

SUMMER

WINTER

AUTUMN

MOON PHASES

2. FIRST QUARTER MOON

3. FULL MOON

1. NEW MOON

4. LAST QUARTER MOON

When we see the moon at night, what we actually see is the reflection of the sun's light on the moon. The moon gets its light from the sun, just like we do on Earth.

The shape of the moon appears to change at different times of the month, gradually moving through its *phases* from a small crescent moon to a half moon to a full moon. Of course, the shape of the moon doesn't really change; the phases of the moon are caused by the moon moving around the Earth so that we see more and more of the portion illuminated by the sun.

Tracing the moon: Ask if you can borrow a calendar with boxes for each day of the month to draw on the phases of the moon. Each night, draw the shape of the moon with colored pencils in the corner of that date. By the end of the month, you will have a complete history of the moon's phases. Hope for clear skies so the clouds won't block your view!

BY THE LIGHT OF THE MOON

SCIENCE TALK

BLOCKED FROM VIEW

On rare occasions, the moon phases between the Earth and the sun, and all three bodies are in a line.

Earth   **Moon**   **Sun**

When this happens, light from the sun is blocked, or *eclipsed*. If the moon completely covers the sun, we have total darkness which is called a total *solar eclipse*. Because of the strength of the sun's rays, *never look directly at the sun during an eclipse*. It is very, very dangerous. Your teacher will show you a way of observing the eclipse without looking at the sun.

If a full moon lines up on the opposite side of the sun, we have what is known as a *lunar eclipse*.

Sun   **Earth**   **Moon**

The Earth blocks the sun's rays, casting a shadow on the moon.

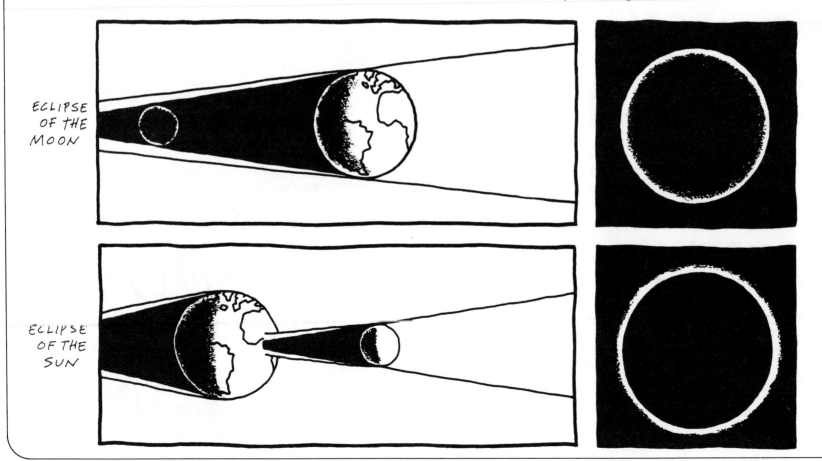

ECLIPSE OF THE MOON

ECLIPSE OF THE SUN

"ONE GIANT LEAP FOR MANKIND"

It's hard to imagine actually walking on the moon, but that's exactly what Neil Armstrong and Col. Edwin E. Aldrin, Jr. did when they landed on the moon on July 20, 1969. Their small space vessel, the Eagle, landed on the Sea of Tranquility during the first of six United States Apollo program moon landings. While this first Apollo mission was on the moon, Armstrong and Aldrin erected an American flag and did many important experiments. They took rock and soil samples for scientists to better understand the moon. When their mission was done, it took the astronauts four whole days to travel back to Earth.

IN FOCUS

STAR LIGHT, STAR BRIGHT

Those beautiful stars twinkling brightly in the night sky are large balls of hot gas, thousands to millions of kilometers around, giving off large amounts of energy from reactions within their interiors. Stars differ from planets in that they are self-luminous, which means they give off their own light (planets shine because they reflect the light from the sun).

Except for the sun, which is the nearest star to us, stars appear only as points of light, even when viewed by the largest telescopes, because of their great distance from the Earth. Our galaxy, called the Milky Way for its creamy appearance in the sky, contains more than 100 billion stars. That's more than you could count in your lifetime!

WHOSE FACE IS THAT?

Look up at the moon and you will see dark markings and shadows that cross the moon's disk. For years people have described imaginary figures such as a lady reading a book, a rabbit with long ears, and, most often, "the man in the moon." The dark markings you see on the surface of the moon are actually rolling plains of land; the bright areas are mountains. Mostly what we see from Earth are darkened craters where pieces of space debris have crashed into the moon, causing deep holes larger than the entire Grand Canyon!

OUT OF SIGHT

TECHNIQUES TOOLS &

Telescopes, tools used by astronomers, make it easier for our eyes to see the planets, stars, and other heavenly bodies by bringing an image into focus and magnifying it for our eyes.

One of the most amazing telescopes, the Hubble Space Telescope named for Edwin P. Hubble, a 20th century astronomer, was launched in April 1990 from space shuttle's *Discovery*. Scientists plan for the telescope to stay in space for 15 years to observe the galaxy.

See for yourself: There are two exciting places to visit to learn more about our universe. An *observatory* has telescopes that you can look through to experience the moon, stars, and planets with a closer view. Many colleges and universities have observatories that are available for public viewing. A *planetarium* creates the feeling of looking up at the nighttime sky. Sitting in a darkened planetarium, hearing about the sky, is an awesome experience. If you visit a big city, ask if there is a planetarium for you to visit.

SOLAR WRAP

Because people have been fascinated by the sun, moon, and stars, they have long been favorite art images.

WHAT YOU NEED

Brown paper bags or butcher paper

Several sponges

Tempera paints

Paper plates

Marker and scissors

WHAT YOU DO

1 Draw a crescent moon, the sun, and a star on some sponges. Be sure the drawings are at least two inches across. Cut out the sponge shapes.

2 Pour tempera paint onto paper plates (separate plate for each color). Dip sponges into paint, and then press onto paper bags that have been cut open or butcher paper, pressing in varied places. Use all one color or several colors for wrap.

CUT OUT SPONGE SHAPES

DIP SPONGES IN TEMPERA PAINTS

THE EARTH BELOW

Would you believe that the ground you're standing on right now may be millions of years old? Or, there may have been an ocean where you are standing that changed the way rocks are layered beneath you. That's the wonderful thing about rocks — they're as different as people are from one another, and they have moved around as much, too. What's beneath our feet can tell us a lot about what the world was like long before people even walked the Earth.

Rock makes up the Earth's *crust*, or shell. Rock comes in all sizes, from little pebbles on the beach to mountain-sized chunks, like the Rock of Gibraltar, near Spain. At very high temperatures, rock melts into a liquid, called *magma*, found at the Earth's *core* (center). Some rocks change from one kind to another, such as quartzite changing into sandstone over thousands of years' time; other substances change into rock from something else entirely such as fine-grained shale formed from mud.

CHANGING  NATURE

We know a lot about what the Earth was like thousands of years ago, because of what scientists have found in the rocky layers of its crust. Geologists, scientists who study the Earth, discovered that it is made of three different kinds of rock:

Igneous (ig-NEE-us) rock, such as granite, forms when magma (liquid rock) cools and hardens. Most magma deep in the Earth cools slowly because the rocks on top of it serve as insulation. (The deeper you tunnel into the Earth, the hotter it gets.)

Metamorphic (meh-tah-MOR-fik) rock, such as marble, changes from one kind of rock to another over a very long period of time, usually because of hot temperatures and pressure deep in the Earth. Lots of times, you'll notice that pieces of metamorphic rock tend to line up in a parallel fashion.

Sedimentary (sed-ih-MEN-tary) rock, such as sandstone and coal, is made from broken down matter (sediment) on the Earth's surface. Over thousands of years, these different kinds of rocks formed layers that geologists study today. Most rock that you find will be sedimentary rock.

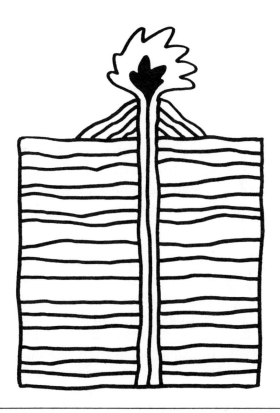

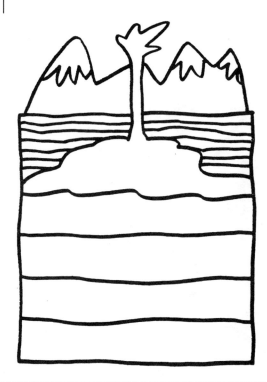

NATURAL WONDERS

THE GRAND CANYON

As you know, big changes in the Earth's surface take a long time to show up. The Grand Canyon in northwest Arizona was created over millions of years. Geologists use the canyon to study layers of rock that were exposed by the cutting force of the Colorado River.

But the Earth is not like a tree whose yearly rings of bark show age. We can't always be sure that the top layers are the youngest, because over millions of years' time, shifts and changes below the Earth might bring old rock up to the surface, pushing younger rocks down beneath them. When this happens, it often causes the rocks to move from one place, like the sea, to another place, such as land. That's why it's possible to find fossils of marine life at the top of a mountain!

MORE · SCIENCE · FUN!

Ask just about anybody and they will tell you they have a special rock. You might have a perfect flat rock that you use for playing hopscotch, or a sparkling rock that you use for a paperweight.

Now you can have a special rock collection and, like a geologist, *sort* and *classify* your rocks according to *size, color, texture,* and *hardness.* Then, if you would like, you can even look up the name of your rocks in a rock identification book from the library.

WHAT YOU NEED

Small paper bag and sandwich bags

Paper and pencil

WHAT YOU DO

1 Ask a grown-up to join you and some friends on a rock hunt. You can go right outdoors around your home or to a park.

2 Pick up small rocks that are of interest to you. Try to find rocks that are different shapes, colors, textures, and from different areas. Do any of the rocks have very unusual shapes from erosion? Do any have fossil markings?

SPECIAL ROCKS

3 Place the rocks you find from each area together in a sandwich bag labelled with the area found.

4 Classify your rocks by hardness (soft rocks are more like chalk), color (do some sparkle or are some marbled), texture (are some smooth and others very rough). Or, you may just want to group your rocks by size.

5 For a temporary collection, place your rocks by groups on a tray covered with a white cloth napkin. For a permanent collection, mount your rocks by group by placing a dab of glue and fastening to a heavy piece of cardboard. If you have identified the kind of rock by name, print the name and where you found it under the rock.

BUTTON UP!

Can you make buttons out of rocks? Well, not exactly, but on the northern shores of Lake Champlain in Vermont, there is a park where rocks do look like buttons. In fact, Button Bay State Park is known for its smooth, water-worn "button rocks" called *concretions*. These concretions are actually sedimentary rocks shaped like buttons — complete with a tiny hole in each center!

The button-shaped disks formed when phosphorus in the lake's water hardened around grasses and weeds, leaving a tiny hole in each button's center where the grass once was. If you held one of these buttons, you could feel for yourself the effects of thousands of years of water-smoothing.

Now I see it: It is fun to look at rocks, twigs, and even mountain-tops as if they were pieces of sculpture. Go for a walk and take along your sharp powers of observation and your imagination. Look for things that occur naturally that remind you of something else. Perhaps you'll see a stone that has been worn into the shape of a duck or a twig that looks like a giraffe or a hammer? If you find the perfect piece of nature's sculpture, bring it home for all to enjoy.

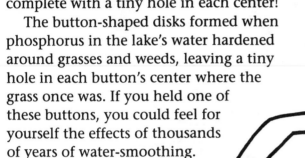

BUCKETS OF SAND

IN FOCUS

Making a beach full of sand can take thousands of years. That's because sand is made of tiny bits of bigger rocks. When water flows over rocks, or when huge ice formations called *glaciers* grind against rocks, little pieces break off. After years and years of banging and rubbing together, the rocks are broken into tiny particles of sand.

You'll find sand in lots of other places, too. Rocks that are on high land are always in a state of deterioration. Over time, gravity, wind, and rain slowly move the broken pieces of rock — or sand — down the grade of land, allowing it to accumulate in oceans, lakes, and other bodies of water. When you see a lot of sand, it's entirely possible that there was an ocean or lake there at one time. Wind is also capable of transporting sand. That's what happens in desert areas where wind freely carries sand to other parts of the land.

Next time it rains, take a walk after the storm has ended. Look at the roadside very carefully. Do you notice a lot of sand near the road's edge? That's where the rainwater transported it and where it settled when the rain stopped.

LONG, LONG AGO

NATURAL WONDERS

Some kinds of rock started out as living things such as plants and animals. You may be surprised to learn that *coal* developed from the remains of prehistoric plants! Limestone rock and coral in the ocean are made up of the shells of huge numbers of tiny animals. The famous Petrified Forest in Arizona is full of rock formations that were once the trunks of trees! *Petrifaction*, meaning "to change into stone," takes place gradually, over millions of years' time, as each pore of a tree is replaced by quartz particles, making the tree denser and stronger than before.

SANDSCAPES

Because sand is really rock being broken into smaller and smaller pieces, sand comes in many different textures. Some sand is rough on your bare feet, and some is as smooth as talcum powder. Depending on the types of rock, sand can be almost pure white, very dark gray, or beautiful pale pink from coral rock. Here's a way to enjoy the beauty of sand right in your home.

WHAT YOU NEED

Containers with lids

Sand or coarse salt

Food coloring

Spoon

Clear, wide-mouthed jar with lid (the straighter the sides, the better)

Knitting needle or pencil

WHAT YOU DO

1 Pour some sand into several containers (coarse salt will work if you don't have any sand), one for each color you wish to use. Leave enough room in the containers to shake up the sand.

2 Drip ten drops of food coloring into a container, put the lid on tight, and shake well until the sand is evenly colored. Add more coloring for a deeper color. Repeat this with other colors for each container of sand.

LID

3 Spoon a layer of colored sand into the bottom of a wide-mouthed jar. Add a second layer of a different color on top; then a third layer, and so on until you've filled the jar to the brim.

4 Gently slide a knitting needle down the side of the jar, through the layers of sand; then slowly lift it out. The sand layers gradually overlap and blend, making an interesting pattern of colorful waves and ripples. (Don't overmix.)

5 Tighten the jar's lid. If you've filled the jar to the very top, your pattern won't be disturbed when the jar is gently moved.

SPOON IN LAYERS OF SAND

USE KNITTING NEEDLE TO DESIGN PATTERNS

WHEN JAR IS FILLED PUT LID ON JAR AND TIGHTEN

A GEOLOGIST'S JOB

IN FOCUS

Geologists have exciting jobs that include many different kinds of responsibilities. They analyze rocks to discover the history of an area, and study earthquakes, volcanoes, and other catastrophic changes in order to predict and lessen their damaging effects.

Geologists also use the Earth as a blueprint for studying the past positions of continents and oceans and to trace previous life through fossils found in rock.

Try it out: You can study the Earth as geologists do by looking for clues about the Earth's history at any rock ledge in your area. If you belong to a scout troop, 4-H group, or the "Y", maybe you can invite a geologist to take you out for some field work. Bring your lab book along (see pages 6 – 7), and study the ledge by standing on the ground, looking up — not standing on top of the ledge, which is dangerous. Is the ledge made up of layers of rock or is it just one thick slab? What kind of rock seems to be on the ground? Is the rock all one color? texture? Are there mountains and hills nearby, or a lake? What clues are there to help you unravel the mystery of the rock ledge?

SUPER SCIENTIST

MAGNIFYING MATTERS

If you've ever looked at a grain of sand — or anything else for that matter — under a microscope, then you already know a lot about two Dutch lensmakers who were actually a father and son, Hans and Zacharias Jansen. You see, about the same time Antonie van Leeuwenhoek was making his simple microscope (see page 14), the Jansens constructed a simple instrument made of two lenses mounted on a sliding tube. This is called a *compound microscope*. Today most scientists still use compound microscopes in their research.

THE EARTH'S CHANGING FACE

Even though many rocks are millions of years old, they wear out and *weather* from years of contact with nature's harsh elements, such as wind and water. Sometimes water gets into tiny holes in rocks too small for our eyes to see. When the weather turns cold, the water freezes and expands, causing rocks to crack and break apart. **Frozen solid & strong as steel:** If you've ever watched waves crash against a rocky shore or a roaring river flow downstream, then you know water is a powerful force. This experiment will show you how strong frozen water is, too.

WHAT YOU NEED

Water

Quart or half gallon milk carton

Duct tape

WHAT YOU DO

1 Fill a milk carton to the brim with water, then tape the end completely. Place the milk carton in the freezer overnight.

2 In the morning, remove the milk carton from the freezer. Examine the carton. Are the carton's sides bent outward? The frozen water expands and takes up more space, pushing the container's sides outward. What do you think might have happened if you used a glass container that doesn't bend? Now imagine what a whole lake full of frozen water can do to a rocky shore!

POUR WATER INTO EMPTY MILK CARTON

TAPE THE OPENING SHUT

FEELING THE HEAT

NATURAL WONDERS

You already know that deep inside its stony crust, the Earth's core is made of hot liquid rock (magma). And there's a good reason why geologists believe magma is pretty powerful stuff. After all, it's what causes volcanoes to erupt.

Volcanoes are mountains with openings or *vents* that reach down in the Earth to where magma is found. Sometimes the heat at the Earth's core or center causes bubbles of *carbon dioxide* gas in magma to get bigger and expand. This expanding gas pushes magma into the vent of a volcano and up to the surface of the Earth. When a volcano *erupts*, or overflows, from the top of the vent, hot lava flows over its sides.

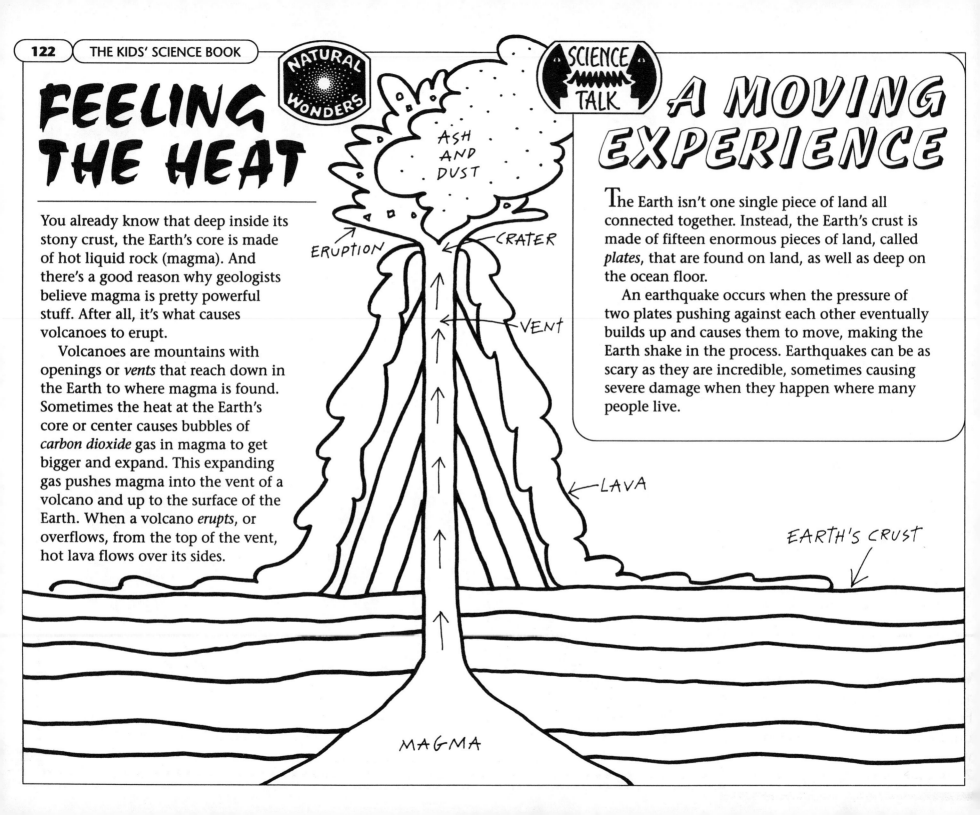

ASH AND DUST

ERUPTION

CRATER

VENT

LAVA

EARTH'S CRUST

MAGMA

SCIENCE TALK

A MOVING EXPERIENCE

The Earth isn't one single piece of land all connected together. Instead, the Earth's crust is made of fifteen enormous pieces of land, called *plates*, that are found on land, as well as deep on the ocean floor.

An earthquake occurs when the pressure of two plates pushing against each other eventually builds up and causes them to move, making the Earth shake in the process. Earthquakes can be as scary as they are incredible, sometimes causing severe damage when they happen where many people live.

MAKE A BLOW-YOUR-TOP VOLCANO

MORE · SCIENCE · FUN!

Make a table-top volcano and actually send fizzy red "lava" down its sides. Make your model as detailed as you like.

WHAT YOU NEED

Salt dough or dirt

Small plastic soda bottle

Baking pan

Red food coloring

Liquid detergent

2 tablespoons (25 ml) baking soda

Vinegar

WHAT YOU DO

1 Line your work area with newspaper, and wear a lab coat or art smock, since this can be messy.

2 With the soda bottle in a baking pan, mold the salt dough into a mountain around the bottle. Don't cover the bottle mouth and be sure not to get dough in the bottle.

3 Fill the bottle almost to the top with warm water mixed with a little red food coloring.

4 Put 6 drops of liquid detergent in the bottle.

5 Add the baking soda, using a curl of paper as a funnel.

6 Pour vinegar slowly into the bottle. Then, watch as a red, foamy mixture quickly rises over the top and flows down the mountain's slopes.

What happened?: When you mix vinegar and baking soda, it makes *carbon dioxide* gas — the same gas that causes the bubbles in a real volcano. The gas bubbles build up in the bottle, forcing the liquid out of the bottle and down the sides of the "volcano."

SALT DOUGH RECIPE

WHAT YOU NEED

6 cups (1.5 l) flour

2 cups (500 ml) salt

4 tablespoons (50 ml) cooking oil

2 cups (500 ml) warm water

WHAT YOU DO

1. Mix ingredients together in a bowl, working it with your hands until smooth and firm. Add more water as needed.

2. Add food coloring if you wish.

BOTTLE MOUTH

DIRT OR CLAY "MOUNTAIN"

LAVA

THE LIGHT OF OUR LIFE

When you turn out the lights at night, it's no surprise that you can't see, but do you know why? It is the reflected light coming into our eyes that makes it possible to see. Without light, we wouldn't see any colors, sparkles, shadows, or reflections in mirrors, either. But light does even more than that.

In fact, without light not only wouldn't we see — we wouldn't be either! Plants need light for photosynthesis (see page 32), and without plants we and the animals we eat wouldn't live. Plant energy is also stored in dead plants as *fossil fuels* such as coal, oil, and natural gas that we use to keep us warm, to run machines, and to produce electricity. Plus the light from the sun heats the Earth and we already know we couldn't survive without that.

Light can come from many places — the sun, a natural source of light, or a lamp or candle, both *artificial* sources of light. So turn on the lights — and your creativity, too — and learn about the reasons for our bright and colorful world!

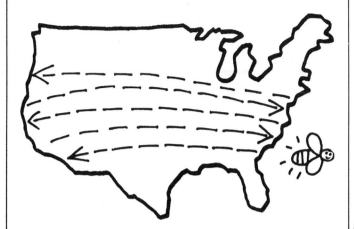

FASTER THAN THE SPEED OF LIGHT!

Exactly how fast is the speed of light? Well, for many years people thought that light traveled at different speeds (as sound does) depending on what its source was and where the observer was. Then, a famous scientist, *Albert Einstein*, proved in his *Theory of Relativity*, that light travels at a constant speed of 186,282 miles (299,792 kilometers) per second. That's like traveling from the east coast to the west coast of the United States over 23 times round-trip in a single second! Whether you shine a flashlight across the room or a lightning bug glows in the dark, the light moves so fast that you can't track its movement.

TOOLS & TECHNIQUES
LIGHTNING CALCULATIONS

You know the safety rules about lightning:

■ Stay indoors or in a car.

■ Never stand under a tree during a thunderstorm.

■ Get out of the water if you are swimming, and stay away from open fields, such as a baseball field or golf course.

■ If you are outdoors and can't get indoors, crouch down in a ball with only the balls of your feet on the ground. Try to get in a ditch so you are not the tallest thing on the ground.

When a thunderstorm is near you, the lightning and thunder seem to happen at the exact same moment. When the storm is further away, you see the lightning before you hear the thunder. What does this observation tell you?

Now, do you want to know how close the lightning is to you? Count the number of seconds between seeing the lightning and hearing the thunder. Divide that number by 5 and you will know the number of miles away the lightning flashed.

SHINING THROUGH

SCIENCE TALK

Have you ever noticed how you can see through some things, such as glass or clear plastic, but not others? Light travels in straight lines that carry light energy in tiny energy packets called *photons*. Clear things like glass or air are *transparent*, which means the lines or *rays* of light pass through them easily. Something you can't see through, like a brick wall, is called *opaque*. You can probably think of lots of things that are opaque. The light rays simply can not get through, so the light is blocked out. But what about tissue paper? You can't really see through it, but when you shine a light on it, the light comes through the paper. This means the light rays have scattered and the material is called *translucent*.

Make a prediction: You can easily test things around your house to see if they are transparent, translucent, or opaque. Try to *predict* what the results will be and then *test* your predictions on a paper napkin, an apple, a glass of water, aluminum foil, and a window screen. What happens to the light in each case? Now shine the flashlight beam into your mouth. Are you opaque, translucent, or transparent? Pretty spooky!

AN ABSENT-MINDED GENIUS

Have you ever forgotten to tie your shoes or put on your coat? Then you've got a lot in common with Albert Einstein. That's right, this famous scientist was very forgetful when it came to the day-to-day details of life, but that didn't mean he wasn't intelligent. Einstein was just a late-bloomer. In fact, he didn't even begin talking with ease until he was nine years old! But Einstein, like all budding scientists, always wanted to know the "whys" and "hows" of things he observed around him. He grew up in Germany, and was even expelled from high school, many say, because he asked too many questions!

FRIGHT LIGHT

Fashion a paper bag to look like a scary Jack-o'-lantern or ghoulish ghost with a translucent glow.

WHAT YOU NEED

Paper grocery bag
Pencil
Scissors
Flashlight
Clay

WHAT YOU DO

1 Flatten the bag on its original creases. With the bag upside down, draw a scary Jack-o'-lantern or ghost face on the front of the bag.

2 Cut out the mouth, nose, eyes, and any other features you want to shine brightly.

3 Stand your flashlight in a base of clay or play dough, and set in the window. Place your paper bag over the flashlight for a glowing face to greet those who dare come near. Make several for table decorations for a Halloween party.

ME AND MY SHADOW

Since light travels in a straight line and can't pass through opaque objects, a shadow appears whenever an object blocks a path of light. That's why your body casts a shadow when you stand between the ground and the sun. Go outside on a sunny day and stand in the shadow of a big tree or a tall building. Do you feel cooler? Of course you do, because the sun's rays aren't reaching you.

How it works: Here's an experiment that will help you understand how shadows are made. Find a flashlight and shine it on a blank wall. Watch how the light from the flashlight travels in a straight line and makes a circle of light on the wall. Put your hand in front of the light. Do you see the shadow of your hand on the wall? The shadow is the dark place where your hand blocks the light.

Move your hand closer and further away from the light. What happens to the shadow? When your hand gets closer to the light, it blocks out more light rays, making a bigger dark place, or shadow, on the wall. Now, try making some hand shadows on the wall with your friends. Have someone hold the flashlight and take turns guessing what each hand shadow is.

You've probably heard of shadow puppets before. Now you know where they get their name. The puppet blocks the light from reaching the wall or "stage," so the audience sees only the puppet's shadow.

WHAT YOU NEED

Stick or rod

White bed sheet

Large box

Scissors and tape

Tag board

Popsicle or craft sticks

Bright desk lamp

WHAT YOU DO

1 Decide on your story and cut out puppets for your characters from tag board. Make them in simple shapes as the audience will only see shadows. Tape each puppet to a Popsicle stick.

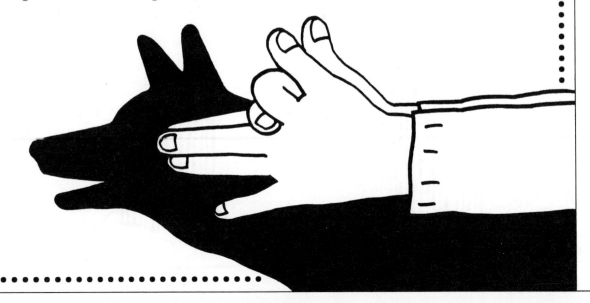

SHADOW PUPPET THEATER

2 Drape a sheet over a stick and hang between two chairs so the sheet hangs as a screen. Set a box on the floor behind the screen to hide your hands during the show.

3 The audience sits in front of the sheet. Puppeteers sit on the floor behind the cartons.

4 Place a bright desk lamp behind the sheet.

5 Hold your puppets (which are opaque) between the light source and the sheet, making shadows. The sheet is *translucent*, so the light not blocked by puppets can pass through it. The audience in front will see the shadows. Move your puppets close to the screen to make giants for your story!

WHERE'S THE COLOR?

AMAZING BUT TRUE

Okay, here's a complicated puzzle for you to figure out. Use your scientific powers of careful observation plus what you already know about light.

Is your favorite red sweater really red or does it just look red?

What a silly question you say! Well, take your red sweater out in the bright sunlight and look at it carefully. Wear it to a grocery store with fluorescent lighting and see if it still looks as red to you. Wear it at night and look at it then. What do you think? If the sweater contained the red color in it, wouldn't it always look exactly the same? The fact is the sweater's color is determined not by the sweater itself, but by the way light bounces off it. If all the light rays bounce off an object equally, the object will appear white. If none of the light waves bounce back, or are reflected back to you, the object will appear black.

Did you ever reach into a pool or deep puddle to pick up a coin? What happens? The coin isn't where it appears to be, and you have to move your hand around a little to locate it. When light enters a transparent material, such as water, it slows down slightly. If it enters at an angle, the change in speed causes the angle to change, bending the beam of light away from its original path.

This process of bending light is called *refraction*, and it has a lot to do with such simple things as finding something in a pool of water, special things like seeing a rainbow, and more complicated things such as how well your eyes work and whether or not you need glasses to help you see better. Science really is everywhere!

Here's a way you can see how light bends for yourself! Draw your observations (something a good scientist often does) and then *compare* your two drawings. What do the drawings show you about light when it travels from air to water at a slant?

BENDING LIGHT

WHAT YOU NEED

Pencil

Glass of water

WHAT YOU DO

1 Fill the glass two-thirds full with water.

2 Place the pencil in the water, holding it straight up.

3 Look through the glass at the pencil. Does the pencil look straight or bent? Draw what you see.

4 Now, lean the pencil against the inside of the glass.

5 Look through the glass at the pencil. Does the pencil look straight or bent? Draw what you see.

6 Compare your two drawings. What can you *infer* from your drawings; that means what is a good explanation for the differences in your drawings based on what you know about light? Good work!

← LOOK THROUGH GLASS HERE

THE COLORS AROUND US

When light travels in a straight line, it appears to be colorless and is called *white light*. When that light bends by passing through a wedge-shaped glass object called a *prism*, it separates into a range of seven colors, called the *visible spectrum*. The longest light waves are deep red, and the shortest are violet. You've seen these seven colors before, as they are the same colors found in the rainbow. Not all light contains the same amount of each color on the spectrum: sunlight has about equal amounts of each color, but some light bulbs have more red and orange, while fluorescent light has more blue and yellow.

A watery prism: By using a mirror and water you can create the wedge-shape of a prism and produce the color spectrum on a piece of paper. Place a mirror in a glass of water at an angle, with the mirror facing the sun. Hold the paper at a slant in front of the glass. Move the paper until the colors show up clearly.

MIX AND MATCH

There is a great variety of color around you. The color of an object depends upon its *pigment* — finely ground chemicals that absorb certain colors of light and reflect others. The colors of paint are due to the pigments they contain.

Did you know that all the colors in the world come from only three pure pigments? These colors — red, blue, and yellow — are called the *primary* colors. Let's suppose you have only red, blue, and yellow paint, but you want to paint a **green tree**. No problem! Just mix blue with yellow. What if you want to paint something orange? Then mix yellow with red. If you want to make a bunch of purple grapes, red and blue will do the trick. Mix all three primary colors together and you'll make black.

A HORSE OF A DIFFERENT COLOR

Have you ever seen a purple horse? What about a green or orange one? Well, get ready to see horses of many different colors!

WHAT YOU NEED

Sheet of white paper

Pencil

Markers (red, yellow, and light blue)

2 pieces picture-frame glass, edges taped

WHAT YOU DO

1 Draw a picture of a horse (or any object you wish) with a pencil.

2 Lay a pane of glass over your picture. On the glass, draw and color in the horse shape with a red marker. Do the same with the other pane of glass, but use a light blue marker.

3 Remove the glass. Color your original picture yellow.

4 Lay the glass with the red horse over the yellow horse. What color is the horse? What happens if you lay the blue horse over the yellow horse? Go to what you know and explain what is happening.

DRAWING ON PAPER—FILL WITH YELLOW

YELLOW

RED

PALE BLUE

CLIMBING COLORS

You know all colors are made by mixing different combinations of the three primary colors — red, yellow, and blue. But did you know there's a way to un-mix colors, too? Try it and see. You won't believe your eyes!

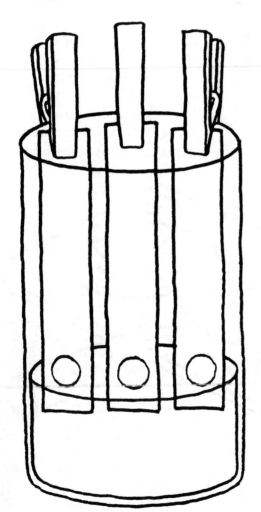

WHAT YOU NEED

White blotter paper or paper towels

Scissors

Water-soluble markers: red, blue, yellow, orange, green, and brown

Tall glass

Wooden spring-type clothespins

Newspaper

WHAT YOU DO

1 Cut the blotter paper into strips, about 4" (10 cm) long and ¾" (.5 cm) wide.

2 Leaving a little white space at the end of the strip, draw solid circles of red, blue, or yellow — one color at the end of each strip.

3 Fasten strips, with the circle-ends down, to the inside of the glass with a clothespin. Carefully pour in just enough water so the white edge of each strip is wet. What happens? As the paper soaks up water, it travels through the circle of color, carrying some of the color with it. Notice the colors on the strips are the same three primary colors.

4 Try three more strips, but this time use orange, green, and brown circles. As the color spreads, you'll see colors that may surprise you. What color does the orange strip show? How about the green and brown strips?

Go to what you know: See page 91, and then go to what you know to explain why only one color climbed up the blotter strips that were colored red, blue, and yellow. Why did more than one color climb up the strips that were colored blue, orange, and brown? Did you notice that the different colors climbed the strips at different speeds? There's a reason for this, too. In making the colors that go into the markers, different chemicals are used. Some of them dissolve in water more quickly than others. The ones that dissolve more quickly are the ones you see moving up the strip first and fastest.

A RAINBOW OF COLORS

NATURAL WONDERS

What do you suppose causes rainbows to appear? Well, you already have the answers, so make an educated guess, or *hypothesis*. You know that sunlight naturally contains all the colors of a prism, which are the same as the colors of the rainbow: red, orange, yellow, green, blue, indigo (dark purplish blue), and violet (reddish purple). (Just remember *Roy G. Biv* to recall the colors in their proper order.) The rest of the science of rainbows you already know, too! Light travels in straight lines when nothing stands in its way. When light passes through a different medium as from air to water, it bends or is *refracted* (this causes the separate colors of a rainbow) and is *reflected* back to the observer, depending on where he or she is standing.

Now think about the experiment you did on page 132. If the sun comes out right after a rainstorm when there are still tiny droplets of rain in the air, the rays from the sun pass through the raindrops. The colors are bent, then separated out and reflected back to our eyes as beautiful bands of color.

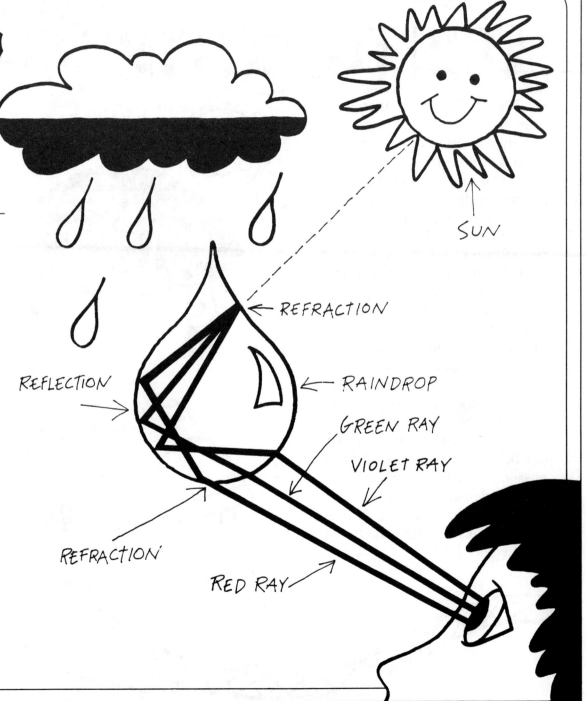

SUN

REFRACTION

REFLECTION

RAINDROP

GREEN RAY

VIOLET RAY

REFRACTION

RED RAY

CATCH THE COLORS!

IN FOCUS

The best time to see a rainbow is when the sun comes out right after a rain shower. To find one, stand with the sun *behind* you and look for a rainbow in the sky. You may even see two rainbows appear in the sky at once! Daytime isn't the only time you can see a rainbow. Look for rainbows at night, too. Sometimes the light from the moon is strong enough to form them.

Make your own: You can make a rainbow with a garden hose by spraying a fine mist in front of you (with your back to the sun). Or, if you are indoors on a cold winter day, make a rainbow by filling a glass of water right to the brim. Set it sticking out just a bit from the edge of a bright sunny window. Place a piece of white paper on the floor and you will see a rainbow of color seem to appear magically. Of course you know it isn't magic at all — it's pure science fun!

BOUNCING BURSTS OF LIGHT

SCIENCE TALK

When you look into a mirror, you see your reflection. And — you guessed it — light makes this reflection possible. Mirrors are made of clear glass with a shiny silver coating painted on the back that *reflects*, or bounces back, the image of whatever is in front of it.   Opaque objects absorb or soak up light; transparent things let light pass through them; shiny things, like the silver coating on a mirror, bounce light back, causing a reflection.

Try placing two mirrors facing each other. Then put an object, such as a small toy, between them. Do you see the endless reflections, caused by light bouncing back and forth between the two mirrors? How many reflections can you count?

INVISIBLE LIGHT

NATURAL WONDERS

Each morning when we wake, we are greeted by the glorious sun. We rely on this *visible light* to see things around us. Without it, we'd be in the dark! As you know, red light has the longest waves, and violet has the shortest.

But there are some kinds of light we can't see at all because our eyes don't register light waves that are longer or shorter than those in the visible spectrum. We say that these colors are *beyond the range* of the human eye. There's *ultraviolet*, which actually means "beyond violet," which has a shorter wavelength than violet. At the other end of the range is *infrared*, or "below red," with light waves even longer than the deepest visible red.

When the sun goes under a cloud, the visible light we see also fades. But not ultraviolet light. It can go right through a cloud without any problem. That's why we can get sunburned on a cloudy day.

MAY THE FORCE BE WITH YOU

We know that, when an apple drops from a tree, it's going to fall down to the ground. We know that the sun will rise every morning and set every evening, because the Earth will keep rotating on it's axis. We don't think about it; we take it for granted.

The reason for these occurrences — and many others — is force. A force is any push or pull on an object — any cause that starts something moving, or stops it, or changes the movement in some way.

Try the experiments ahead and you'll understand why apples fall down, why the Earth keeps going around the sun, and lots more, too.

NATURAL WONDERS

WHAT WOULD YOU WEIGH ON ANOTHER WORLD?

Get on a scale and check your weight. Let's say it's sixty pounds — is that what you'd weigh anywhere in the universe? If you were on the moon, the scale would say you weigh less than ten pounds. On giant Jupiter, though, you'd weigh 175 pounds! On tiny, faraway Pluto, you'd barely move the dial of the scale, to three pounds, clothes and all.

SCIENCE TALK

IT'S A MATTER OF GRAVITY

Why would your weight change as you went through the solar system? Because when a scale gives your weight, what it's really telling you is how much your body is being pulled downward by a force called *gravity*. Gravity pulls things toward the center of Earth — or any other planet, or even any object. As a rule, the bigger the object, the stronger its gravity. So Jupiter, the biggest planet, would pull on you a lot harder than Pluto, the tiniest, and the scale would show the difference. You wouldn't change, but the *force of the gravity* pulling you downward would.

All objects, no matter how small, have at least a little gravity. Even a pebble does — but it's so slight, we can't feel it. Gravity keeps the Earth and the other planets orbiting around the sun, and it keeps the moon in orbit around the Earth.

GALILEO

Galileo (gah-luh-LAY-oh), who lived from 1564 to 1642, is an all-time super scientist. Before Galileo, it was thought that a heavy object would fall faster than a light one. According to legend, he went to the top of the famous leaning tower of Pisa (yes, it really does lean!) and dropped two items of different weights. They hit the ground together, proving that gravity pulls all objects to Earth at the same rate of speed.

FREE FALL

You know gravity pulls everything on Earth downward. Do you think gravity pulls a heavy object faster than a light object? Can you think of a way to find out?

WHAT YOU NEED

Partner (if there's one handy)

Chair

Sheet of newspaper

2 oranges

Grape (or green pea, or other very small object)

WHAT YOU DO

1 Stand on the chair with an orange in each hand and have your partner kneel, so he or she can watch the oranges hit the floor (cover floor with newspaper, please).

2 Drop the oranges *from the same height at the same time* onto the newspaper. What do you observe? The oranges are your *control*.

3 Now, from the chair, drop the orange from one hand and the grape from the other, making sure to drop them both at once from the same height. What happens? Are you surprised? What can you and your partner conclude from your observation?

Conclusion: Gravity pulls all objects downward at the same speed, regardless of their weight.

STARTING AND STOPPING

Have you ever been in a car that had to stop suddenly? As the car slowed down, you were thrown forward against your seat belt. When the car starts forward, you feel like you're pushed back into your seat.

Have you ever seen the kind of roller coaster where the track does a complete loop? How come people don't fall out when they're upside down?

The answer to all these questions is *inertia* (in-URH-sha). All things have inertia, which means this: when something is still, inertia keeps it still, unless a force puts it in motion; when something is moving, inertia keeps it moving, and in the same direction, unless a force makes it stop or change direction.

When your car comes to a quick stop, the brakes stop the car, but they don't stop you. Inertia makes your body keep going forward, until your seat belt stops you as well (which is why wearing a seat belt is very important).

When a car's engine makes the car go forward, your body wants to stay put, which is why you get pushed back into your seat.

It's the same on a loop-the-loop roller coaster. As the coaster car starts up the inside of the loop, inertia keeps the riders in the same line they've been moving in. The result is that they get pushed down into their seats — lucky for them!

SCIENCE TALK

SPINNING IN PLACE

As the Earth moves around the sun, gravity and inertia control its orbit. The Earth's inertia causes it to tend to move in a straight line, while the sun's gravity pulls the Earth toward it. The result is that the Earth is pulled into a distinct, nearly circular orbit around the sun.

Make your own orbit: This is an outdoor experiment. Tie a rope to the handle of a pail filled with tennis balls or other light objects. In an open space, hold the pail by the rope and swing it over your head. As long as the pail keeps moving, everything will stay in it, even when it's upside-down.

When you whirl the pail around, it's like you're the sun, the pail is the Earth, and the rope is the sun's gravity, tugging the pail toward you. Why doesn't anything fall out of the pail while it's in motion? Inertia makes the pail and its contents want to go in a straight line, away from you.

MOVING MARBLES

Inertia means that a rolling ball on a smooth, level surface will roll forever if nothing stops it. (In fact, friction and air pushing against the moving ball will eventually bring it to a stop.) But interesting things happen when a motionless object gets in the way of a moving one. Try this and see for yourself.

WHAT YOU NEED

Two long straight pieces of wood (yardsticks work well)

Tabletop or floor

Tape

Six or more marbles of equal size

WHAT YOU DO

1 Tape the sticks to the tabletop so they're parallel and about 1/2" (1 cm) apart.

2 Put two marbles in the middle of the track between the sticks, several inches apart.

3 Flick a marble so that it rolls and hits the other one. What happens to the two marbles? The one that had been rolling stops. The one that had been still now rolls! The momentum of the rolling marble transfers to the other one, stopping the first and setting the second in motion.

Momentum can transfer from one object to another.

4 Now put two marbles on the track so they touch, and a third several inches away. Flick the single marble into the other two. This time, the rolling marble stops, the middle one stays put, and the third one rolls. The momentum went through the second marble into the third. The amount of momentum is only enough to move one marble at the speed of the first marble.

Momentum can pass from one object, through a second, and into a third.

5 Try other combinations: two marbles into three still marbles, or three into three. You'll find that however many marbles you set in motion, the same number will be made to roll when they're hit.

The total amount of momentum at the beginning will stay the same.

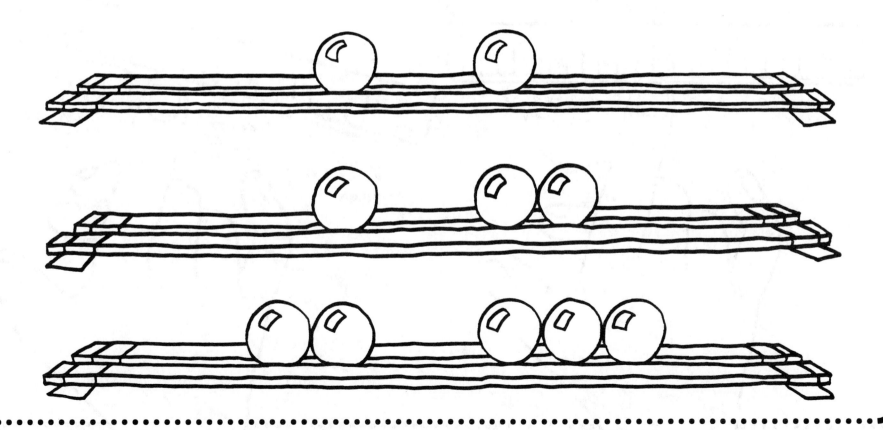

BALANCING ACT

Have you ever seen a tightrope walker balanced on a wire at a circus? To *balance* is to arrange weight so that it stays put — even on something as narrow as a wire — despite gravity's trying to pull it down.

Can you balance a ruler on your finger? Give it a try. If you do, you'll see your finger is right under the middle of the ruler. That's what's called the ruler's *center of gravity*, or *balance point* — where if supported it will stay balanced, or in *equilibrium*.

The weight of the balanced ruler is evenly divided, half on either side of its balance point. With your finger under the center of gravity, gravity can't make the ruler fall. If you move your finger, even a little, so it's no longer directly under the balance point, the ruler tilts to the side where the center of gravity is now, and down it goes.

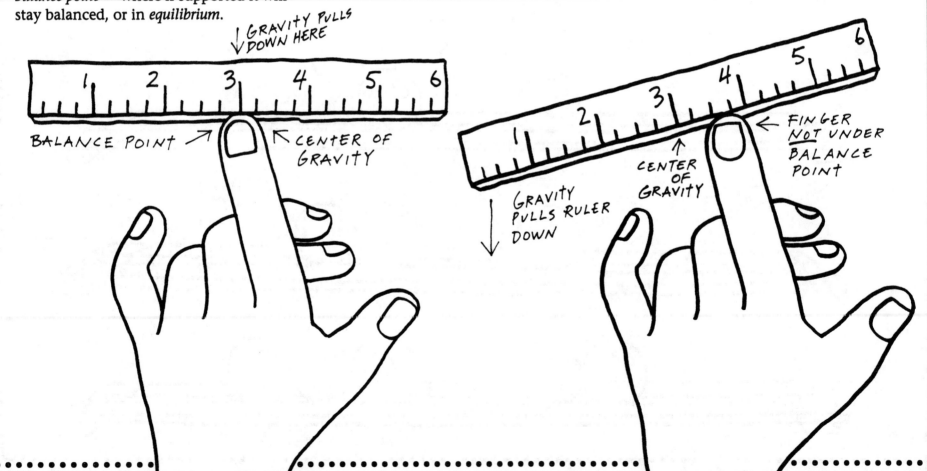

THE POWER OF THE MAGNET

Another important force is *magnetism*. Like gravity, magnetism is invisible — you can't see it, although its effects are all around you. There's a big difference between the forces: gravity works on all *matter* — everything is pulled by it. But magnetism only works on some things, and not on others. How can you find out what a magnet will pull, and what it won't?

Figure it out: Gather together a large number of items made of all different substances: glass, plastic, wood, paper, different kinds of metal, and so forth. Try touching each with a magnet. Separate the items into two groups: those that stick to the magnet, and those that don't. What is similar about the things in each pile? What makes the piles different? What can you conclude about which materials are affected by magnets, and which are not?

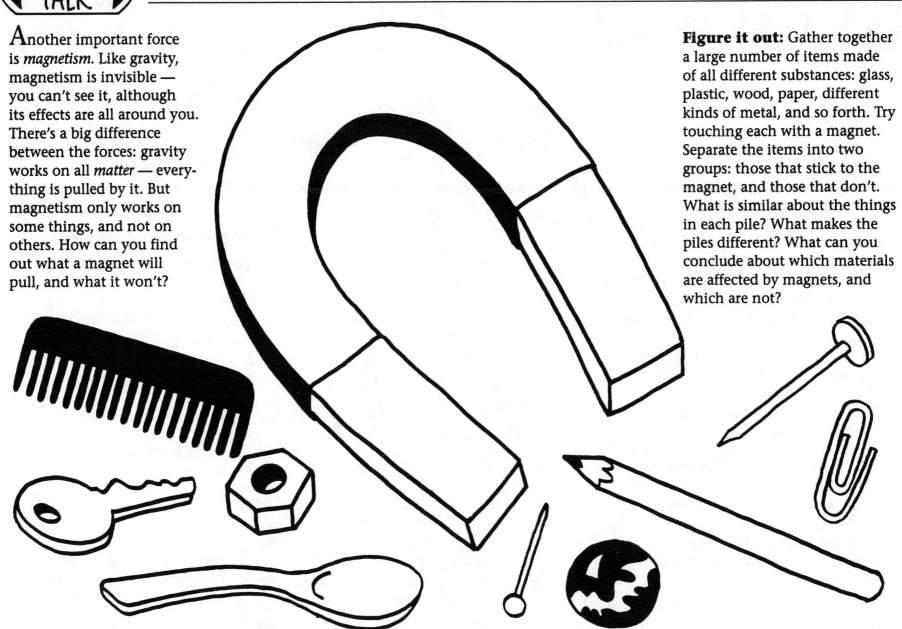

MAGNETS PULL, BUT THEY'RE PICKY

IN FOCUS

If you decided that a magnet won't attract wood, paper, plastic, or ceramics — you're right! The only material that magnets attract is metal. And not just any metal: many metals, such as lead, aluminum, copper, and tin, aren't affected by magnets, either. The metal most likely to be pulled by a magnet is iron. Steel, which is made from iron, and mixtures of metals that include iron are also attracted by magnets.

All magnets have a *north pole* and a *south pole*. Some magnets — especially the long kind called bar magnets — are marked "N" and "S" at the ends to tell which pole is which. Try placing the north or south poles of two magnets together, and they push each other away. Place the north pole of one against the south pole of the other, and they stick like glue. Opposite poles of magnets attract each other: north to south. But similar or *like* poles — north to north, or south to south — repel each other. That's the rule on magnets: "*Like poles repel, and unlike poles attract*." Do you suppose the expression "opposites attract" started with magnets.

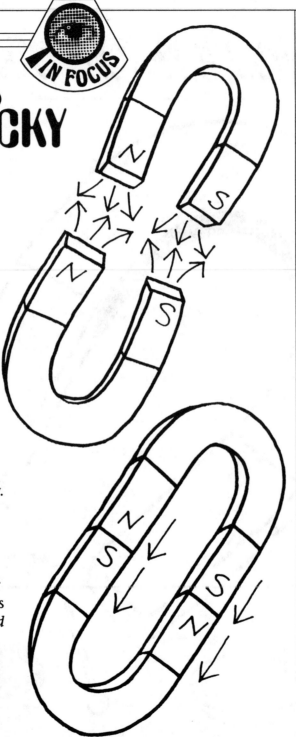

Making these cat magnets is a fun way to see magnets work. Sometimes these cut-out kitties want to stick together; sometimes they don't.

WHAT YOU NEED

Small, strong magnets (available at art and craft stores)

Thin cardboard or index cards

Scissors

Tape

Markers, crayons, or paint

WHAT YOU DO

1 Draw the outlines of the cats on the cardboard and cut out. Decorate as you wish.

2 Draw and cut out two pairs of legs for each cat. Cut notches in the bodies and legs, as shown.

3 Cut an oblong base for each animal, longer than the animal's body and wide enough for the legs to fit.

HELLO, KITTY – GOODBYE, KITTY!

4 Put the animals together by fitting the leg notches into the body notches. Fold the bottoms of the legs into "paws" and tape paws to the base.

5 Tape a magnet to each animal, either in front of its front legs or behind its rear legs. Put the animals together on a smooth surface and watch what happens.

TAPED ON MAGNET

BASE

TAPE DOWN PAWS ON BASE

cut NOTCH

LEGS (cut 2)

FOLD FOR PAW

FOLD FOR PAW

CUT NOTCHES →

FIT LEG NOTCHES INTO BODY NOTCHES

WHERE DO THEY COME FROM?

NATURAL WONDERS

The very first magnets people found were pieces of rock that naturally attracted iron. The rocks were called *lodestones*. We call the mineral of which lodestones are made *magnetite*. And we still don't know why magnetite is naturally magnetic!

Making a magnet: If you can pick up a piece of metal with a magnet, you can then turn that metal into a magnet, too. Just rub the metal 10 to 15 times in the same direction with one end of a permanent magnet. The stronger the magnet you use, the longer your new magnet will keep its power. Try it with nails, screws, and other metal objects. But don't be surprised if the metal loses its power after a while.

Have you used a compass while walking or hiking? Compasses are instruments people use to help them determine their direction while traveling. All a compass is — we bet you already know! — is a free-swinging magnetic pointer on a dial. Since the pointer is a magnet, it will always point to the north. Here's how to make your own.

WHAT YOU NEED

Index card

Compass

Scissors

Bar magnet

2 sewing needles and thread

Tape, pencil

Wide-mouthed jar

WHAT YOU DO

1 Cut an index card in half the short way, making two 3" x 2.5" (7.5 cm x 6.25 cm) pieces. Fold one piece in half lengthwise.

2 Ask a grown-up to stick a (knotted) threaded needle through the center of the fold. Remove the needle from the thread.

HOMEMADE COMPASS

3 Rub the needle 12 times, *in the same direction, from eye to point, with the north pole of a bar magnet.* Do the same thing with a second needle of the same size. Now, you've turned both needles into magnets.

4 Open the folded card, and tape a needle on each inside fold, so the needles are parallel and pointed in the same direction. Refold the card as it was before.

5 Tie the end of the thread in the card around the middle of a pencil so the card hangs no more than 2" (5 cm) beneath it.

6 Place the pencil across the mouth of a jar with the card hanging freely inside. Make sure the card isn't stuck against the side of the jar. The card will swing around; mark "N" on the card when it points north. Move the jar or the card around, and watch the card return to the same position. The card will always point north, until the needles lose their magnetism.

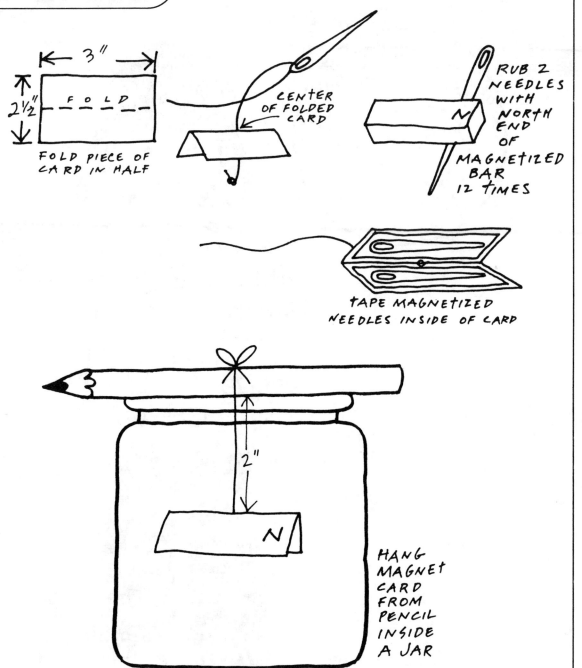

3"

2½"

FOLD

FOLD PIECE OF CARD IN HALF

CENTER OF FOLDED CARD

RUB 2 NEEDLES WITH NORTH END OF MAGNETIZED BAR 12 TIMES

TAPE MAGNETIZED NEEDLES INSIDE OF CARD

2"

HANG MAGNET CARD FROM PENCIL INSIDE A JAR

ALL THE WORLD'S A MAGNET

AMAZING —BUT— TRUE

What's the biggest magnet on Earth? Actually, the biggest magnet on Earth is Earth! That's right, the Earth really is a gigantic magnet, with its own magnetic force. Like all magnets, it has a north and a south pole, too. The north and south *magnetic* poles are not exactly the same as the *geographical* north and south poles, but they're very close. All magnets, if allowed to swing freely, will end up with their south poles pointing toward the Earth's magnetic north pole (see page 148).

Which way's north?: Tie a bar magnet with a clearly marked north pole to a string so it hangs evenly balanced. The magnet's south pole will come to rest pointing to the Earth's magnetic north pole. Compare it with a compass, and you'll see!

MORE MAGNET MATTERS

More • Science • Fun!

Will a magnet work from a distance when it's not actually touching the piece of metal? Are all magnets the same strength? Here's a way to answer both of these questions.

WHAT YOU NEED

Paper clips

Sheet of paper

Pencil

Magnets of different sizes and shapes

Ruler

WHAT YOU DO

1 Lay a sheet of paper on a flat surface and put a paper clip on it. Make a mark where you placed the clip.

2 Set a magnet a few inches away from the clip. Move the magnet closer very slowly. Make a mark to show where the magnet was when it pulled the clip to it and measure the distance between marks.

3 Try the same thing with different magnets. You'll find some magnets are stronger than others and, therefore, will pull from farther away than others. But they all can pull on iron and steel, even when they're not touching.

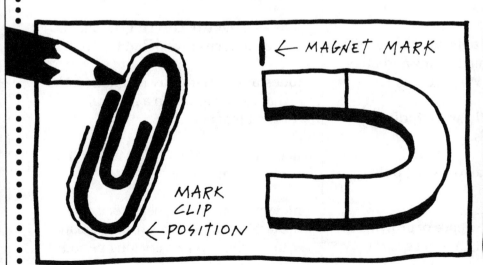

MARK CLIP POSITION

← MAGNET MARK

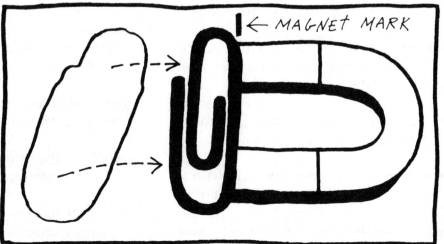

← MAGNET MARK

albumen — the white of an egg.

camouflage — concealment by means of a disguise. Certain animals are camouflaged in the wild.

capillary action — the process by which a plant stem carries liquid upward.

carnivorous — subsisting or feeding on only meat.

chalazas — the white filaments that anchor the yolk of an egg.

chlorophyll — a chemical in green plants used in photosynthesis.

Chordata — the phylum containing all animals with backbones.

cold-blooded — having a body temperature that changes according to the temperature of the surroundings.

compound microscope — a microscope with two lenses mounted on a sliding tube.

concave — a lens that curves inward, making objects look smaller.

concretion — sedimentary rocks with a hole in the center shaped by water.

contamination — the process of making something dirty, infected, or polluted.

control — the part of an experiment that stays the same.

convection cell — a cycle of air movement in which warm air rises, replacing cooler air.

convex — a lens that bulges outward, making objects look bigger.

embryo — an animal in the early stages of growth and development, before birth or hatching.

equator — the imaginary circle around Earth that divides our planet into two equal parts called hemispheres.

equilibrium — a state of being balanced.

fluorescent — bright and glowing; emitting electromagnetic radiation absorbed from some other source.

galaxy — one of the billions of systems in the sky that contains stars and other matter; the Milky Way is our galaxy.

geologist — a scientist who studies rocks and minerals.

gravity — the natural force that pulls objects downward.

hydroponics — the science of growing plants without soil; they are grown mainly in water.

hypothesis — an educated guess, based on available facts, made by a scientist who is trying to predict what will happen.

igneous — a type of rock, like granite, that forms when magma cools and hardens.

immiscible — the property by which two liquids, such as oil and water, separate into layers.

inertia — a property of matter that keeps it at rest or in motion unless acted upon by another force to change the situation.

infrared — lying outside of the visible spectrum of light at the red end.

invertebrates — animals that do not have backbones.

lens — a piece of curved glass that is used to focus rays of light.

lodestone — naturally magnetic rocks that can be found in a mineral called magnetite.

magma — liquid rock that is found in the core of Earth.

metamorphic — a type of rock, like marble, that changes from one kind to another over a very long period of time.

mollusk — one of a large group of animals that usually lives in water and has a hard outer shell.

momentum — the force or speed of an object when it is moving.

nutrients — food substances that provide nourishment to a living thing.

observatory — a place with telescopes for viewing the stars and planets.

omnivore — an animal that eats both plants and animals.

opaque — blocking the passage of light.

orbit (*n*) — the path an object takes around a sphere.

phase — the appearance or shape of the moon at regular times in a cycle.

photon — a tiny unit of intensity of light energy.

photosynthesis — the process by which green plants use energy from the sun to produce food.

pigment — finely ground chemicals that absorb certain colors of light and reflect others.

plates — the huge, movable pieces of Earth's crust.

prism — a wedge-shaped piece of glass, a raindrop, or other transparent material that refracts, or bends, light into the colors of the rainbow.

procedure — the step-by-step method of accomplishing something, such as an experiment.

refraction — the bending of light.

regeneration — the process of creating something again.

sedimentary — a type of rock, like sandstone, that is made from broken down material on Earth's surface.

seed coat — the protective outer part of a seed.

self-luminous — giving off its own light.

sphere — a rounded shape, like a ball.

spinnerets — tiny tubes at the rear of a spider's body that produce silk.

toxic — poisonous.

translucent — permitting some light to pass through, such as a sheer curtain.

transparent — clear; permitting light to pass through completely.

transpiration — the process by which plants release water vapor.

tuber — the fleshy, underground root or stem of some plants, such as the potato.

variables — things that change in an experiment.

vertebrates — animals with backbones.

visible spectrum — the range of seven colors in light.

warm-blooded — having a constant body temperature independent of the temperature of the environment.

white light — light traveling in a straight line that appears to be colorless.

zoologist — a scientist who studies animals.

BOOKS

Astronomy. Robin Kerrod (Lorenz Books)

Bill Nye The Science Guy's Big Blast of Science. Bill Nye (Addison-Wesley)

Explorabook: A Kids' Science Museum in a Book. John Cassidy (Klutz Press)

Exploring the Science of Nature (series). Jane Burton/Kim Taylor (Gareth Stevens)

Hands-On Science (series). (Gareth Stevens)

The Highlights Book of Science Questions That Children Ask. Jack Myers (Barnes & Noble Books)

The House of Science. Philip R. Holzinger (Wiley)

Light Fundamentals: Funtastic Science Activities for Kids. Robert W. Wood (McGraw-Hill)

Magnet Science. Glen Vecchione (Sterling)

Making Things Change. Gary Gibson (Copper Beech Books)

Measure Up With Science (series). Brenda Walpole (Gareth Stevens)

Questions and Answers about Weather. M. Jean Craig (Four Winds Press)

Rocks & Minerals. Steve Parker (Dorling Kindersley)

A Scholastic Kid's Encyclopedia — Science. David Rubel (Scholastic)

Science Arts. Mary Ann Kohl and Jean Potter (Bright Ideas for Learning)

The Science Book. Sara Stein (Workman)

The Science Discovery Book. Anthony D. Fredericks, Brad K. Cressman, and Robert D. Hassler (Scott, Foresman)

Science Facts. Steve Setford (Dorling Kindersley)

Science Wizardry for Kids. Margaret Kenda and Phyllis Williams (Barron's)

Science Works! (series). Steve Parker (Gareth Stevens)

Simple Science Projects (series). John Williams (Gareth Stevens)

Start Collecting Fossils. Ted Daeschler (Running Press)

Super Science Concoctions. Jill Frankel Hauser (Williamson)

Toy Box Science (series). Chris Ollerenshaw and Pat Triggs (Gareth Stevens)

VIDEOS

Earth: Geology of an Ever-Changing Planet. (United Learning)

Gravity. (Lucerne Media)

Light Science: You Can Do It! (Encyclopædia Britannica Educational Corporation)

Magnetism. (United Learning)

The Plant World. (United Learning)

Rocks, Minerals, and Fossils. (Barr Films)

Science Essentials: Geology. (Encyclopædia Britannica Educational Corporation)

Science Essentials: Plants. (Encyclopædia Britannica Educational Corporation)

Science Essentials: Weather. (Encyclopædia Britannica Educational Corporation)

Science Fair Projects. (Beacon Films)

Science Rock. (Kimbo Educational)

The Scientific Method. (Barr Films)

Weather. (DK Vision)

What Is Science? (Encyclopædia Britannica Educational Corporation)

Carnegie Science Center
One Allegheny Avenue
Pittsburgh, PA 15212

The Exploratorium
3601 Lyon Street
San Francisco, CA 94123

Manitoba Museum of Man and Nature
190 Rupert Avenue
Winnipeg, Manitoba R3B 0N2

Maryland Science Center
601 Light Street
Baltimore, MD 21230

Miami Museum of Science
3280 South Miami Avenue
Miami, FL 33129

Museum of Science
Science Park
Boston, MA 02114

Museum of Science and Industry
57th Street and Lake Shore Drive
Chicago, IL 60637

Ontario Science Center
770 Don Mills Road
Don Mills, Ontario M3C 1T3

Science Center of British Columbia
1455 Quebec Street
Vancouver, British Columbia V6A 3Z7

Science Museum of Minnesota
30 East Tenth Street
St. Paul, MN 55101

Science Place
1318 Second Avenue
Dallas, TX 75210

www.mala.bc.ca/~mcneil/sci.htx

www.hiwaay.net/cwbol/weather.html

www.discovery.com

www.nationalgeographic.com

www.edisonx.com/kids/

www.windows.umich.edu/photoscience.
laasu.edu/photosyn/study.html

A

acid rain 80
alligators 61-62
animal kingdom 44-73
  alligators 61-62
  characteristics of 44
  chimpanzees 48
  cold-blooded 55, 61
  crocodiles 61-63
  endangered 54, 63
  fish 55-60
  Homo sapiens 45
  insects 66-71
  invertebrates 47
  kingdom 44-45
  mammals 50, 55
  reptiles 61-63
  spiders 71-73
  turtles 61, 63
  vertebrates 47, 56
  warm-blooded 50, 55
  whales 50-54

B

butterflies 66-70

C

cells
  convection 94
  regeneration 65
chimpanzees 48
class, *Arachnida* 71
classification
  of animals 47
  a hunt 46

of rocks 114-115
in science 45-46
color 130-136
  experiments with 132-134
  light and 130
  pigment 132
  primary 132, 134
  prisms 132
  rainbows and 135-136
compasses 150-152
crocodiles 61-63

D

distance
  between planets and sun 99-100
  measuring 99

E

Earth
  age of 112
  day and night 102
  description of 101
  distance from sun 99-100
  eclipses seen from 108
  magnetism of 152
  model of 101
  moving plates of 122
  orbit of 103, 106, 143
  rock types 113
  rotation of 102, 103
  seasons on 106
  speed at equator 103
earthquakes 122
eclipses 108
eggs
  examining insides of 8
  shell, growing seeds in 34-35

endangered species 54, 63

F

fish 55-60
forces 138-153
  gravity as 139-141, 147
  inertia and 142-145
  magnetism as 147
  natural occurrences and 138
  weight and 139
fossils 114

G

gravity
  balance and 146
  center of 146
  Earth and 143
  experiments 140-141
  as a force 139-141, 147
  Galileo (Galilei) and 140
  strength of 139
  and the sun 139
  weight and 139

H

hypothesis 16-17, 84, 135

I

inertia 142-145
insects 66-71
invertebrates 47

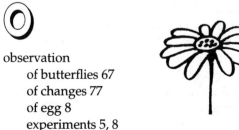